# THE NEW
# PENNSYLVANIA PRIMER

LUCILLE WALLOWER

*Assisted by*

BERNICE WIER

**PENNS VALLEY PUBLISHERS**
Harrisburg, Pennsylvania
1984

# PREFACE

**THE NEW PENNSYLVANIA PRIMER** is the well known basal text for boys and girls in the elementary grades, updated to the times and with additional stories of particular interest. Also added is a section on black history and an updated chapter on the state today that is of special use to the teacher.

To introduce each story to the children, the teacher will find the *Words to Know* at the end of each chapter, of great value. These words can be presented visually and talked about. The *Word Meanings* list will also help to liven each child's interest.

After each chapter is a list of *Things To Do*. These activities will not only help to teach a history lesson, but will bring into use art, music, science, and geography.

**THE NEW PENNSYLVANIA PRIMER** will stimulate the interest of both teacher and pupil in the unusually varied and often exciting history of our Commonwealth.

---

## PENNS VALLEY PUBLISHERS
Harrisburg, Pennsylvania

Copyright, 1984
ISBN #0-931992-48-6
*All Rights Reserved*

Printed in Pennsylvania, U.S.A.

# CONTENTS

## PART I

## THE BEGINNINGS OF A STATE AND A NATION

1. Indians of Pennsylvania . . . . . . . . . . . . . . . . . . . . . 3
2. The Founding of Pennsylvania . . . . . . . . . . . . . . . 13
   William Penn in England . . . . . . . . . . . . . . . . . 13
   William Penn's Great Treaty . . . . . . . . . . . . . . . 17
   The Walking Purchase . . . . . . . . . . . . . . . . . . . 20
3. People Who Came to Pennsylvania . . . . . . . . . . 28
   Ephrata Cloisters . . . . . . . . . . . . . . . . . . . . . . . 31
   Moravians of Bethlehem . . . . . . . . . . . . . . . . . 34
   Frenchmen at Azilum . . . . . . . . . . . . . . . . . . . 36
   Ole Bull's Norwegian Colony . . . . . . . . . . . . . 38
4. George Washington's Dangerous Trip . . . . . . . . 43
5. The Battle of Bushy Run . . . . . . . . . . . . . . . . . . 56
6. The Liberty Bell's Story . . . . . . . . . . . . . . . . . . . 63
7. Betsy Ross and the Stars and Stripes . . . . . . . . . 69
8. A Bitter Winter at Valley Forge . . . . . . . . . . . . . 74

# PART II

# INTERESTING PEOPLE IN PENNSYLVANIA

9. A Legend About John Harris ................ 83
10. Molly Pitcher with Washington's Army ........ 90
11. Benjamin Franklin and the Making of America .. 97
12. Benjamin West: The Boy Who Liked to
    Paint Pictures ........................ 103
13. James Forten: Black Sailmaker Extraordinary... 109
14. Lucretia Mott and The Battle Against Slavery .. 117
15. John James Audubon: Painter of Birds
    and Animals .......................... 126
16. Stephen Girard: Richest Man in America ...... 135
17. Stephen Foster and His Songs the
    Whole World Sings .................... 140
18. James Buchanan: A Boy Who Became
    President ............................ 146
19. George Westinghouse: A Great Inventor ....... 153

## PART III

## THE STRUGGLE OF THE BLACK MAN

20. Beginnings of Slavery and the Slave Trade .....158
21. Slavery in Pennsylvania and the New Nation....163
22. The Battle for Freedom....................168
23. The Struggle for Dignity ...................173

## PART IV

## THE LAND AND THE PEOPLE

24. Old and New Ways of Travel in Pennsylvania ...182
25. How People Live and Work in Pennsylvania ....192
26. Symbols of Our State .....................205

Rare Book Dept. of the Free Library of Phila.
The Famous Treaty Elm of long ago at the Harbor of Philadelphia
(see Chapter 2)

# PART I

# THE BEGINNINGS OF A STATE AND A NATION

PA Historical and Museum Commission

Lopowinso, a Delaware Indian chief

# 1. INDIANS OF PENNSYLVANIA

LONG AGO the Indians were the only people who lived in this country. Only Indians lived in the land we call, Pennsylvania. They lived here long before the white man came.

Most Indians had dark copper-colored skin, browned by the sun. They had straight black hair and black eyes. The men of some tribes shaved their heads and left just a tuft of hair in the middle. The women wore braids.

There were different groups, or tribes, of Indians. The Seneca Indians lived in northwest Pennsylvania. The Nanticokes lived in the east. The Shawnees were scattered through the state. The Susquehannocks lived along the Susquehanna River. The Delawares lived near the Delaware River. There were other tribes, too. Do you know some of their names?

In those days, Pennsylvania was mostly forest land. The Indians lived in small villages in the forest. Around the Indian village was a fence. The fence was made of tall poles to keep out wild animals.

Each Indian family lived in a wigwam. The wigwam was round. It was made of young trees. The outside was covered with pieces of tree bark.

4                                    PENNSYLVANIA PRIMER

PA Historical and Museum Commission
Statue of a famous Pennsylvania Indian chief, Shikillamy

There were no windows in the wigwam. A hole at one side, covered with deerskin, was the door. Inside the wigwam, the Indian family was safe from wind, rain, and snow.

There were no cupboards or closets. The Indians hung their clothes on poles. Dried corn and other dried foods were hung from poles, too.

Around the inside walls of the wigwam was a low bench. This was the bed. All the family slept here. In winter, the family slept on the floor near the fire.

Sometimes, two or three or more Indian families lived together. They lived in a longhouse. A longhouse was just like its name. It was a wigwam made longer. Each family had its own room.

Everyone in the Indian village had work to do. The men built the wigwams. They made tools from sharp stones, shells, and wood. They made canoes from trees. The men had to be good hunters and fishermen. The Indians needed meat and fish for food. There were no food stores in those days!

The Indians needed animal skins to make clothes. There were no clothing stores!

Dresses for the girls and women and shirts and breeches for men were made of deerskin. Moccasins were made of deerskin, too. Rabbit furs were used to make a warm robe to wear. A soft bed could be made from a bear skin.

Every Indian village had a chief. The chief was chosen by the people. An Indian boy wanted to be strong. He wanted to be brave. He wanted to be wise. When he grew up, perhaps he would be chosen chief of the village!

An Indian girl helped her mother. Indian women were busy all day long. They gathered wood for the fires. They cleaned the fish and meat. They stored food away to eat the next winter.

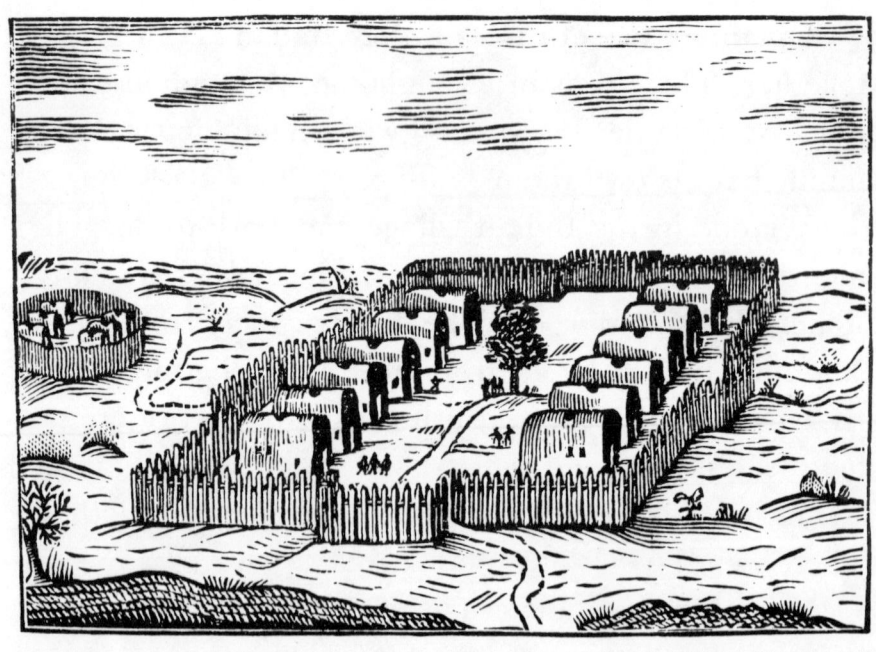

Rare Book Dept. of the Free Library of Phila.
Old drawing of a Delaware Indian village

Indian women planted and cared for the crops. The Indians raised many vegetables. Indians were the first people of America to grow corn. They made corn meal cakes, mush, and other foods from corn.

The Indian women made clothes from animal skins. They made baskets from grasses. From clay they made dishes and jars. The women carried all the water, took care of the children, and cooked all the meals.

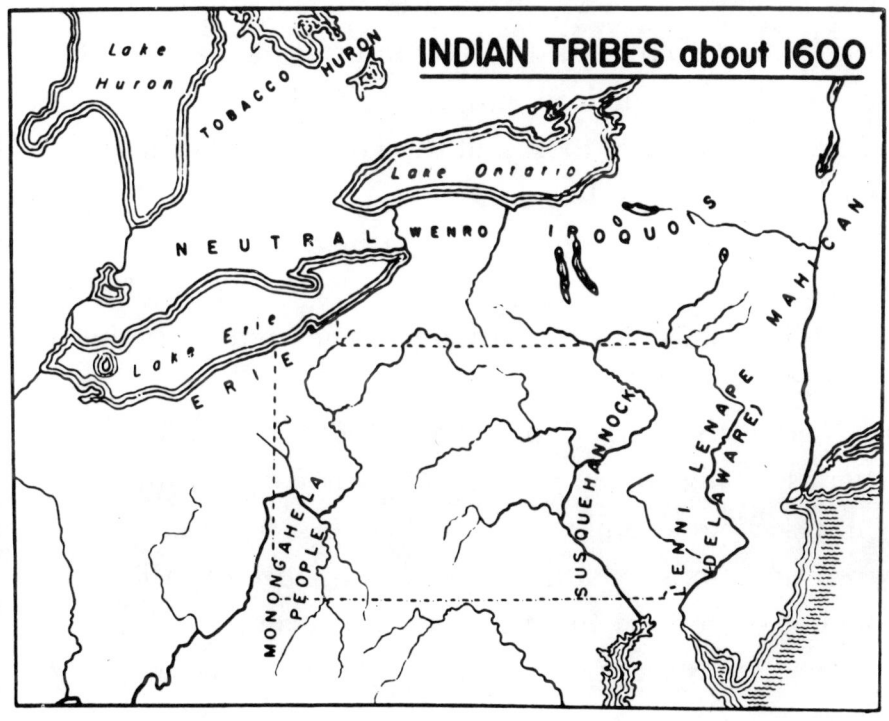

Indian children did not go to school. But they learned to write a sentence in pictures. They made signs with their hands. Indian children were taught to be polite. They were kind to older people. Indian children were obedient.

Indians called each month a "moon." They told time by the sun and moon. They knew directions by the sun or the stars. Indians called God the "Great Spirit."

Indian men liked to go to council meetings. They liked to hear stories. They played games and took part in special dances. They liked the music of drums and rattles and chants. But of course most of the time they hunted and fished to supply their village with food. They shared their food and the land they claimed with each other as one big family.

The Indians had many footpaths through the forest. When the white men came, they used these same Indian trails for roads. The Indian taught the white man how to live in the forest.

Today there are more than 5,500 Indians living in Pennsylvania. They are of different tribes from many places. They live like other people, but try to keep their own traditions. Near Philadelphia is a group called the United American Indians of the Delaware Valley.

In Pennsylvania, there are towns, rivers, and mountains called by Indian names. What places with Indian names do you know?

INDIANS OF PENNSYLVANIA 9

Just think! Perhaps there was an Indian wigwam where your house stands now! Perhaps Indian boys and girls played games on your schoolground!

## WORDS TO KNOW

| | | |
|---|---|---|
| braids | Indians | Shawnees |
| chief | longhouse | Susquehannocks |
| council | moccasins | trails |
| crops | Nanticokes | tribe |
| Delaware | Pennsylvania | village |
| Great Spirit | Senecas | wigwam |
| | shaved | |

## WORD MEANINGS

| | |
|---|---|
| chief | Leader or head man of a tribe. |
| council | A group of persons called together to give advice and discuss or settle questions. |
| moccasins | Soft shoes, often made of deerskin, worn by American Indians. |
| obedient | Doing what one is told. |
| wigwam | A hut of poles covered with bark or skins, made by American Indians. |

## THINGS TO DO

1. At the beginning of the study of THE NEW PENNSYLVANIA PRIMER, it is suggested that a large

outline map of the state be prepared. It could be made on either cloth or heavy paper and hung in the room, so that as the study develops, rivers, mountains, cities, etc. can be added to the map. A committee of children who like to draw might add small pictures to show people, places, and events. The size of the pictures should be in proportion to the size of your map, keeping the map clear and uncrowded, but giving an artistic over-all effect by the time the whole study is completed. This map could be very handsome. It would introduce geography, art, and history, and would be a project in which all the children would take an interest.
2. On the map draw a few bark huts and several Indians in places where the Indians lived. (See the Historical Wall Map of Pennsylvania, published by Penns Valley Publishers.)
3. Build a small model of a bark hut or a longhouse from pictures in reference works.
4. Write a short story using pictures for as many words as possible—Indian style.
5. Make a list of towns, rivers, streets, schools, etc. that have Indian names in your county or region.
6. The Indians made up interesting stories about the stars. They thought they formed pictures in the

sky. Look for the stories of the Big Bear and the Little Bear constellations.
7. If you live where you can visit an historical museum, you will enjoy seeing the arrowheads, spearpoints, baskets, and pottery the Indians made.
8. Make a list of all the Indian tribes in Pennsylvania. Also list where the different tribes lived.
9. Make an Indian doll family. Make them some winter clothes.
10. Make a list of foods the Indians ate, and see if you can prepare an Indian dish such as corn meal mush.
11. Learn an Indian dance.
12. Read a book about the forest Indians. Some good books are:
    Brewster, Benjamin. *The First Book of Indians,* (Franklin Watts, Inc. 1950).
    Slaughter, William A. *Little Turtle of the Lenni Lenape,* (Franklin Printing Co., 1931).
    Deming. *Red People of the Wooded Country,* (Laidlaw, 1932).
    Wallower, Lucille. *Indians of Pennsylvania, Workshop* (Penns Valley Publishers, 1976).

PA State Dept. of Commerce
William Penn, founder of Pennsylvania

# 2. THE FOUNDING OF PENNSYLVANIA

### WILLIAM PENN IN ENGLAND

MANY YEARS ago a boy named William Penn lived in England. His father was an important man in the King's Navy; he was called Admiral Penn.

William liked to study. He went to a boys' school. Later, teachers taught him at home. When William became a young man, his father sent him to a fine school. But William would not go to the church meetings at school. So he was sent home. Admiral Penn was very angry.

At this time in England, everyone was supposed to attend the Church of England. That was the law. But some people held church meetings of their own. One group of these people called themselves "Friends." Other people called them "Quakers."

A Quaker would not go to war. He wanted to be friends with all men. A Quaker said "thee" and "thou" to all persons. He would not bow to other people, even to the lords of the land. He would not take off his hat to anyone, not even to the King. Quakers acted this way because they believed all men are equal in the sight of God.

When William was a boy, he heard Thomas Loe, a Quaker, preach. He never forgot what Thomas Loe said. After leaving school, William tried to please his father. But then he heard Thomas Loe preach again. He decided to be a Quaker, too.

William went to Quaker meetings. He preached about being a Friend, so he was put into prison. There he wrote books about the meaning of religion and about the events of his time. Now Admiral Penn loved his son very much. He paid a fine of money so that William was set free from prison.

Then William tried to please his father. He studied to be a lawyer. Soon after this Admiral Penn died.

King Charles II owed William Penn's father a great deal of money. After the Admiral died, the money was owed to William. The King did not have the money but he owned much land. William asked the King to give him land instead. He asked the King for a piece of land in America. George Fox, the great Quaker leader, had told William about the beautiful land along the Delaware River. William wanted the land to make safe homes in America for the unhappy Quakers.

King Charles II liked Admiral Penn's son. He gave him the land in America.

# THE FOUNDING OF PENNSYLVANIA

"I will call the land *Sylvania,* meaning woodland," said William.

"The land shall be called *Pensilvania*—Penn's Woods," said the King. "It is named in honor of your Father." Today we spell the name of our state, Pennsylvania.

The King sent a message to the people who lived on this land in America. A few people from the countries of Sweden, Holland, and England had already settled in the province. The King told these people to obey the new governor, William Penn.

Then Penn wrote a friendly letter to the people. He told them that they would be free to worship God as they pleased. He told them that they would help to make their own laws. He invited unhappy people in many countries to come live in Pennsylvania. Governor Penn also wrote a friendly letter to the Indians. Before long, he sent his cousin to the province to take care of business matters.

Then one day William Penn sailed from England. With him were about one hundred people. They sailed in the little ship *Welcome.* After two months at sea, the *Welcome* reached America. Penn landed in Pennsylvania at a place now called Chester. It was late in October in the year 1682.

A few days later Penn sailed up the Delaware in a barge. The barge was a small boat with a crew of eight men, six to man the oars. Penn landed at the place he had chosen for a city.

William Penn stepped ashore. "This, then, is Philadelphia," he said, "the City of Brotherly Love. It is to be a green, country town."

William Penn's Manor House, called Pennsbury, on the Delaware River
PA Historical and Museum Commission

# THE FOUNDING OF PENNSYLVANIA

## WILLIAM PENN'S GREAT TREATY

William Penn was very happy to be in his province. The people were glad that he had come. Penn visited his Quaker friends. He walked, talked, and ate with the Indians. In games, he could run faster and jump farther than many of the Indians!

During these busy days Governor Penn carefully planned the city of Philadelphia. He planned wide streets and beautiful parks.

There were not enough houses for all the settlers. Some of the people lived in caves along the river bank. Ships from England brought nails, tools, and workmen. More log houses were built. William Penn's house was built of bricks. Later he gave this house to his daughter Letitia. You can see it today in Fairmount Park in Philadelphia.

Penn built a much bigger house for himself and his family. It is called Pennsbury Manor. This house is in the country in Bucks County along the Delaware River above Philadelphia. Today, it too, can be visited.

Governor Penn wanted the Indians and the people in his province to be friends. One November day in 1682, the Indian chiefs gathered under a big elm on the banks of the Delaware River. They came to meet the governor.

Rare Book Dept. of the Free Library of Phila.
An old drawing of Penn's first landing in Philadelphia

They wore their finest deerskin and bright feathers. They sat in a half circle around the council fire. The chiefs sat in front. The old men sat on either side. Back of them sat the young men, then the Indian women, called squaws, with their children.

Governor Penn came to the meeting in a barge. With Penn were the men who helped to govern the province. They stepped out of the barge to the river bank and walked toward the council fire. They carried chests filled with gifts for the Indians.

# THE FOUNDING OF PENNSYLVANIA

William Penn was tall and handsome. He was finely dressed in honor of the event. Around his waist he wore a sky blue sash to show that he was the governor.

Under the elm the men spread the gifts. There were blankets, mirrors, guns, and knives for the men. There were beads, kettles, and hoes for the women. There were many other things the Indians liked.

The Indian chiefs and the Englishmen smoked the pipe of peace. Then William spoke: "The Great Spirit knows that I am your friend. The white men and the Indians should help each other like brothers." Then the Indians talked among themselves.

A chief stepped forward. He took Penn by the hand. He said, "We will live in love with William Penn and his children as long as the creeks and rivers run, and while the sun, moon, and stars will shine."

The chief gave Penn a wampum belt. It was made of small, white shell beads. In the center are the figures of two men made of violet-colored beads. One is a white man. He is wearing a hat. The other is an Indian. They are clasping hands. You can still see this wampum belt at the Historical Society of Pennsylvania in Philadelphia.

Philadephia grew from a green, country town into a big city. There is a giant statue of William Penn on top of City Hall tower. You can visit Penn Treaty Park.

William Penn made his dream come true. In Pennsylvania everyone may choose his own church. When you are grown up, you may help to choose the men to govern the state. William Penn was a wise and good man. His ideas helped to make a nation of free people, the United States.

## THE WALKING PURCHASE

In 1686 the Indians gave William Penn a deed to land along the Delaware River. This land was to be located north of present-day Wrightstown in Bucks County extending "as far as a man could go in a day and a half." This would be about twenty miles a day through forest and swamp.

By 1737 this land was needed for new settlers. William Penn was no longer living. His sons, John and Thomas, and James Logan, President of the Pennsylvania Council, asked the Indians to decide the matter. At last four Delaware Indian leaders signed the deed. The land now belonged to the Penns. But how much land was "as far as a man could go in a day and a half"? The land had to

# THE FOUNDING OF PENNSYLVANIA

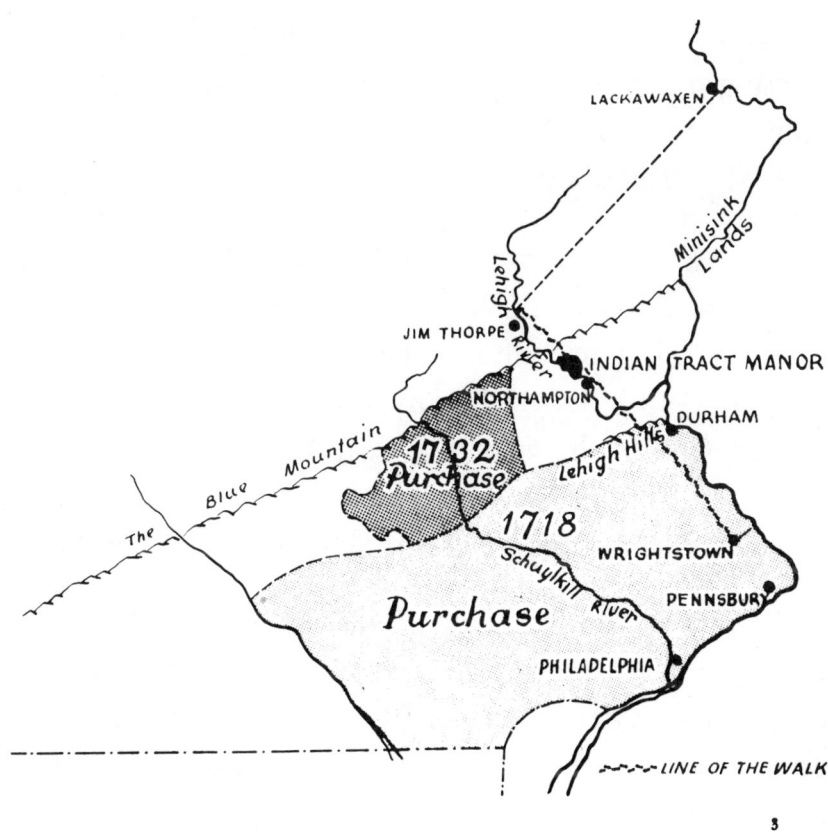

be walked off. James Logan hired three men to make the walk. They were Edward Marshall, James Yeates, and Solomon Jennings. The Penns offered money and five hundred acres of land to the man who walked the fastest and farthest.

On September 19, 1737, the walkers and three

Indians met at a large chestnut tree near Wrightstown meetinghouse. A crowd of people gathered at the starting point. Along the way, other persons waited with food for the walkers.

At first, the white men just walked. Then they walked faster and faster.

"Walk, don't run!" cried the Indians.

In two and a half hours, at Red Hill, Jennings and two Indians could not walk any more. The other Indian named Combush, went on with Marshall and Yeates. Near what is now the city of Bethlehem, Combush sat down to rest a moment, then was too tired to get up.

By sunset Marshall and Yeates arrived on the north side of Blue Mountain. At sunrise the next morning, they started again. At the foot of the mountain, Yeates grew faint and fell. Marshall helped him until another person came. Then he ran on by himself. At noon, the walk was to end. By that time, Marshall had reached a spot on Broad Mountain near the present-day town of Jim Thorpe. It was about sixty miles from the starting point. This was almost three times farther than the Indians thought it would be.

The Indians knew that they had been cheated. They thought, however, that the boundary line would run from the town of Jim Thorpe straight across to the Delaware River. Instead, a slanting line was made far up the river, taking in much more land. Also, the Penns gave presents to the Iroquois Indians. They asked the Iroquois to make the Delaware Indians move off the land. The Iroquois were much stronger than the peaceful Delawares.

The Delaware Indians had loved William Penn. However, the sons of William Penn were not like their father. For seventy-three years there was peace in Pennsylvania. But the Delawares never forgave the sons of William Penn for the way they had been treated. When the French and Indian War started, the Delawares, who had always been friendly, turned against the settlers.

## WILLIAM PENN IN ENGLAND

### WORDS TO KNOW

| | | |
|---|---|---|
| Admiral Penn | honor | province |
| Chester | King Charles II | Quakers |
| Church of England | message | *Welcome* |
| governor | Philadelphia | William Penn |
| preach | | worship |

## WORD MEANINGS

admiral     Officer of the highest rank in the navy.
governor     A man who rules a state or province.
message     Words sent from one person to another.
province     A part of a nation or kingdom.

## WILLIAM PENN'S GREAT TREATY

### WORDS TO KNOW

| | | |
|---|---|---|
| chests | peace | statue |
| clasping | sash | treaty |
| elm | squaw | United States |
| ideas | | wampum |

### WORD MEANINGS

chest     A large box with a lid and usually a lock.
elm     A tall, graceful shade tree.
squaw     An American Indian woman.
treaty     An agreement between groups or nations.

# THE FOUNDING OF PENNSYLVANIA

## THINGS TO DO

1. Make a mural of Penn's life. You could display it in a hall of your school.
2. Plan a play about Penn and Charles II, or Penn and the Indians.
3. Make a Quaker hat.
4. Build a model of a barge like the one Penn used. Pack it with gifts for the Indians.
5. Learn an Indian song.
6. Draw the elm tree on your map of Pennsylvania to show where William Penn and the Indians signed the Peace Treaty. Perhaps you would rather draw a small figure of William Penn.
7. Draw a picture that shows William Penn and the Indians making the Peace Treaty.
8. Go to see a Quaker meetinghouse. Find out more about how the Quakers worship.
9. William Penn and the Indians had pledged to live in peace "as long as the creeks and rivers run and while the sun, moon, and stars still shine." After the "Walking Purchase," this peace ended. Learn more about the ways white settlers got land from the Indians who lived in Pennsylvania.

## THE WALKING PURCHASE

### WORDS TO KNOW

| | | |
|---|---|---|
| boundary | Iroquois | meetinghouse |
| deed | Jim Thorpe | purchase |
| Delawares | John Penn | Thomas Penn |
| James Logan | | Wrightstown |

### WORD MEANINGS

deed — A record of a transfer of property.
meetinghouse — A place for worship.
purchase — To buy.
boundary — A line that shows the limits for a piece of land.

### THINGS TO DO

1. In the "Walking Purchase" the land was measured by Indian fashion. How do we measure these things: distance, time, cloth, eggs, coal, butter, milk, potatoes, temperature, electricity, precious stones, and land?
2. Mark the route of the "Walking Purchase" on the class map.

# THE FOUNDING OF PENNSYLVANIA

3. A pedometer measures the distance covered in walking. Use one on a hike. You can walk a mile. Can you walk five miles?

PA Historical and Museum Commission
Johan Printz, Swedish governor of first colonies on the Delaware

# 3.   PEOPLE WHO CAME TO PENNSYLVANIA

## FROM THE OLD WORLD TO A NEW ONE

AFTER AMERICA was discovered, other men wanted to see this New World. A Dutchman was the first person to sail a boat up the Delaware River. The Dutch, from the country of Holland, were the first European people to settle in the land we call Pennsylvania. The Dutch traded with the Indians, but only a few built homes here.

Then people from Sweden, another country, came to live on an island in the Delaware River. They made friends with the Indians. The Swedes were the first people to build a log cabin in America. These log cabins were like their homes in Sweden. The Swedish people were farmers. They liked this country and built homes here.

A few years later England claimed this land. King Charles II gave William Penn a huge part of it along the Delaware River. This made Penn very happy. Now he and his Quaker friends could go to Pennsylvania. Hundreds of Quaker families left England and Wales. They made new homes in and near Philadelphia.

# PEOPLE WHO CAME TO PENNSYLVANIA

Penn also wanted to help people from other countries. He had papers printed telling about his land in America. He invited all unhappy people to come live in Pennsylvania.

In the country of Switzerland and in parts of Germany, as in England, it was the law that everyone must go to the state church. Some people did not want to do this. They did not believe in fighting, either. So they fled to Holland and other parts of Europe. But there were always wars in Europe. These German-speaking people came to live in Pennsylvania.

A cozy room of early Pennsylvania German settlers

PA State Dept. of Commerce

The first German people to come to Penn's Woods settled near Philadelphia. They called the place Germantown. Soon thousands of German people came to Pennsylvania. Most of these Germans were farmers. They cut down the trees and cleared the land. The rich soil made good farm land. They built big barns very much like the ones they had left in Germany. The Germans were hard workers. Sometimes these people are called Pennsylvania Dutch.

Over 200 years ago the Amish people came from Germany, Switzerland, and Holland to Pennsylvania. Today the Amish live and dress very much as their ancestors did then. They are farmers and peace-loving people. You can see their beautiful farms near Lancaster and in parts of central Pennsylvania.

In Ireland there were people who had first come from Scotland. They were called Scotch-Irish. They were not happy either. They too came to Penn's land. Many Scotch-Irish people made their homes in western Pennsylvania. Some people from France and other countries also came to live here.

In those days, the ships that sailed the ocean were not very big. A ship did not have motors; it had sails. The wind made the ship move. Sometimes it took two months to cross the ocean! Well-to-do people brought many things with them—horses, cows, or furniture for a new home, but more often all a family could bring was packed in one or two trunks.

Many people left dear homes, loved friends, and relatives. Because of their beliefs, they were willing to face danger. They wanted to help make the laws that governed their lives. They wanted to worship God as they pleased. They wanted the right to work and to make a good life for themselves. So they came to Pennsylvania.

The first law to be made in Pennsylvania said that everyone may worship God as he pleases. This was a new idea in those days. Many people who believed the same things wanted to live together in the same place. Some of their settlements seem strange to us today.

## THE EPHRATA CLOISTERS

One group of people from Germany settled in the forests of Lancaster County. They called themselves Brothers and Sisters, and wore long robes and hoods which they wove themselves. The log houses they built were very large. The Brothers' House was for men. The

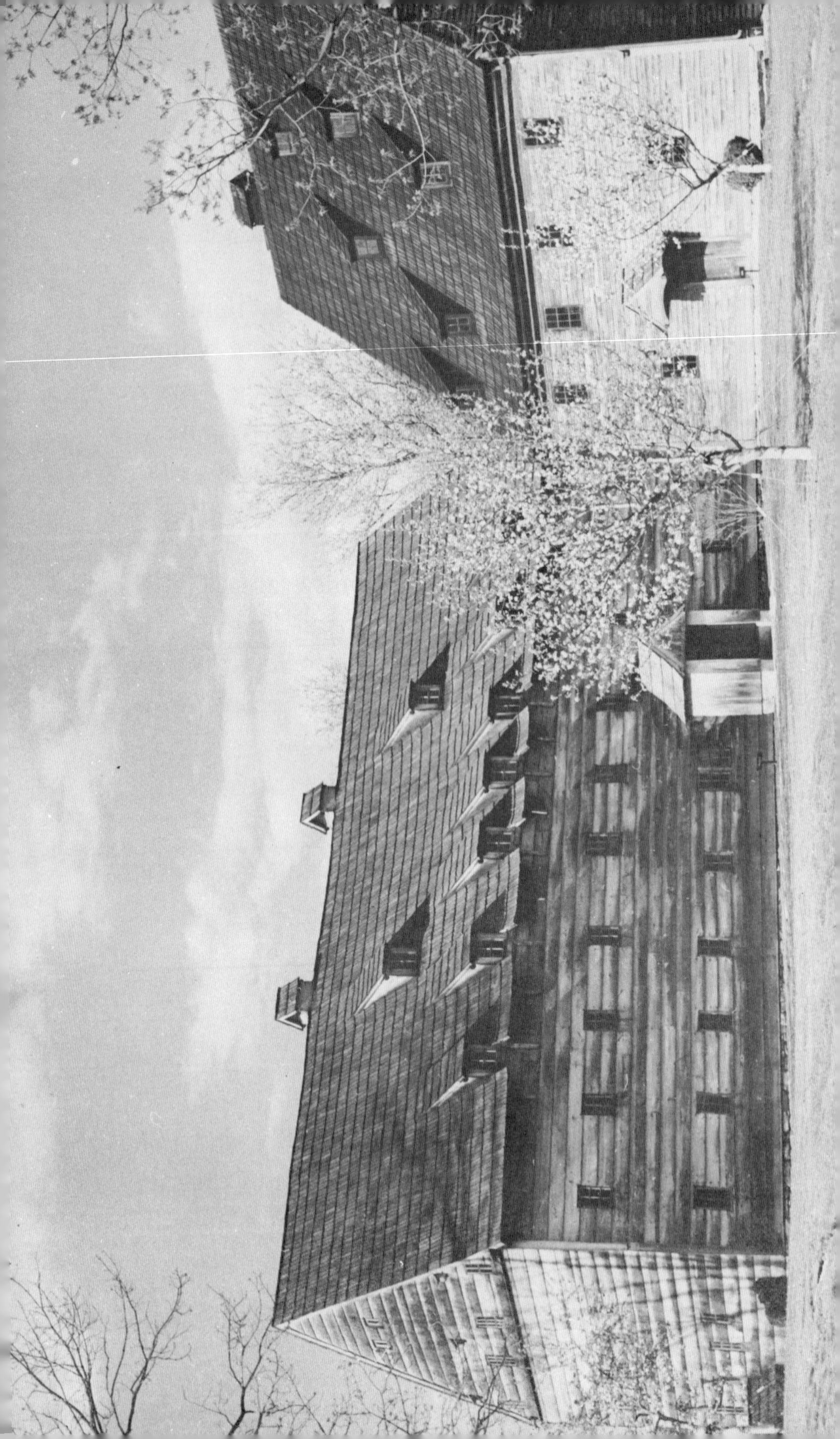

# PEOPLE WHO CAME TO PENNSYLVANIA

Sisters' House was for women. Each had a chapel. This place was called the Ephrata Cloisters. Families did not live in the Cloisters. They lived in a nearby village.

Together these people built a big log church. It was said to be the largest building in America at that time.

The Brothers and Sisters spent all their time at work or at prayer. Each had a task to do. The Brothers farmed the land. They had a flour mill, a bakery, and a shoemaking shop.

Several of the Brothers were printers. They printed some of the finest books in early America. The Brothers made the paper and the ink. They made the leather covers from animal skins for the books.

The Sisters were busy spinning and weaving cloth. They also wrote the music of songs in little books. They painted flowers and birds around the music. The beautiful way the Brothers and Sisters sang hymns has never been forgotten.

A few of these buildings still stand. You can see how these people lived in 1740. The town that grew nearby is called Ephrata.

Buildings at Ephrata built over 200 years ago

## THE MORAVIANS OF BETHLEHEM

Another group of people, the Moravians, came from Germany. There they had lived on the land of a friend, a nobleman. His name was Count von Zinzendorf.

These people also called themselves Brothers and Sisters. The men wore plain dark suits. The women wore white aprons over full skirts, and white caps tied under the chin with ribbon. The children dressed like their parents. Little girls wore red ribbons in their caps.

The Moravians built a log cabin in the forest near the Lehigh River. One room was a chapel; the other room was a stable. The first of these people lived upstairs in the attic.

That first year, the men hunted for food. The women planted a vegetable garden. And they made friends with the Indians.

In the winter of 1741 Count von Zinzendorf came to visit the Brothers and Sisters. How glad they were to see him! This made their first Christmas in the New World a very happy one.

On Christmas Eve the Moravians sang hymns in the chapel. They could hear the animals in the next room. A cow mooed. A horse neighed.

Taking a lighted candle, Count von Zinzendorf rose. He led the way to the stable. As he walked, he sang a

Dresses worn by Moravian girls

well-loved hymn.

Then he said, "We are here to remember the Christmas story. In honor of that story, let us call this place Bethlehem."

The town of Bethlehem grew very fast. Other Moravians came across the sea from Germany. Big houses of yellow stone were built. The Moravians taught the Indians about God. They taught them how to read and write.

For a hundred years only Moravians lived in Bethlehem. Then people from other countries came here to live. Today Bethlehem is a city. A huge mill makes steel for all the world—steel for little things like pins and needles, and steel for big things like ships and airplanes.

The old stone houses still stand in the same place. The Moravians still hold their beautiful church services. At Easter and Christmas people come from all over the world to worship in Bethlehem, Pennsylvania.

## FRENCHMEN AT AZILUM

South of Towanda, Pennsylvania, there is a beautiful valley. The Susquehanna River, winding through the valley, looks like a silver-blue ribbon. From the river rises a huge stone. Some people call this place Standing Stone.

# PEOPLE WHO CAME TO PENNSYLVANIA

In the fall of 1793 a group of people came to this valley. They had come from France, a country far across the ocean. There was war in France. Many French people did not want the King and Queen to be the rulers of France.

The people who fled to Pennsylvania were friends of the royal family. If they had stayed in France, they would have been put in prison or killed. Here in Penn's Woods these French people were safe. They called the valley *Azilum,* which means a hiding place.

The French people were not used to living in the forest. They knew nothing about cutting down trees or building houses. They paid other men to do this work.

The French wanted good roads, beautiful gardens, orchards, and fine animals. They liked pretty clothes and pretty things for their houses. They had picnics and went boating on the river. The French did not want to live like rough backwoods people.

The name of the French Queen was Marie Antoinette. The people of Azilum hoped that she would come safely to America. They built a big house for her. But, alas, she never escaped from France. Both the King and the Queen were killed.

Later, most of these French people went back to their own country. They loved France very dearly. But some of the families stayed in the New World. Today, in northeastern Pennsylvania, you can find towns named after these families. In the museum at Azilum there are things from the French village and a model of the place. The state has recently purchased this land. Perhaps you know some boys and girls whose ancestors came from France.

## OLE BULL'S NORWEGIAN COLONY

Norway and Sweden are two countries across the ocean. They are close together. Years ago, the people of Norway were told to obey certain laws which some people did not like. One of these people had the odd name of Ole Bull. He was a famous violinist. Ole Bull had traveled in America giving violin concerts. Everywhere people liked to hear him play.

Ole Bull liked this country. He dreamed of making a new home here for the unhappy people of Norway. So Ole Bull returned to America and bought land in northern Pennsylvania. He invited people from his country to come to "New Norway" to live. In 1852, several hundred people from Norway came to Kettle Creek Valley.

Little villages of log cabins were soon built. Ole Bull planned to build a castle high on a rock above his land.

PEOPLE WHO CAME TO PENNSYLVANIA

He made many fine plans for new Norway. His dreams did not come true, however. The wooded hills and valleys were pretty but not good farming land. And there were other misfortunes. Soon the settlers went back to Norway. Only a few families stayed in Pennsylvania.

Today this land is Ole Bull State Park. The flags of Norway and the United States fly on the hill where the castle was to stand. Some people say that you can still hear the music of Ole Bull's violin in Kettle Creek Valley!

## FROM THE OLD WORLD TO A NEW ONE
### WORDS TO KNOW

| Amish | Holland | Scotland |
| England | Ireland | Sweden |
| France | laws | Switzerland |
| furniture | Norway | trunks |
| Germany | relatives | Wales |
|  | sails |  |

## WORD MEANINGS

| | |
|---|---|
| relative | Father, brother, aunt. cousin, etc. |
| sail | A piece of cloth spread to the wind to make a ship move through the water. |
| trunk | A big box for holding clothing, etc., when traveling. |

## STRANGE AND INTERESTING SETTLEMENTS

### WORDS TO KNOW

| | | |
|---|---|---|
| ancestors | Ephrata Cloisters | orchards |
| Azilum | hymns | printers |
| bakery | Kettle Creek Valley | settled |
| Bethlehem | Marie Antoinette | spinning |
| castle | misfortunes | stable |
| chapel | Moravians | steel |
| Count von Zinzendorf | Ole Bull | weaving |

### WORD MEANINGS

| | |
|---|---|
| ancestors | Your father, your mother, your grandfathers. |
| hymns | A song in praise of God. |
| misfortune | Bad luck. |
| stable | A building where horses or cattle are kept. |
| steel | A hard, strong metal. |

## THINGS TO DO

1. Build a miniature log cabin.
2. On your map of Pennsylvania, show where the Swedes, Germans, Scotch-Irish, etc., settled.
3. Paint or crayon the flags of France, Germany, Norway, and Sweden.
4. Find out more about Marie Antoinette.
5. Visit the Ephrata Cloisters, Ole Bull State Park, or Bethlehem. Collect pictures and leaflets about such places.
6. From what country or continent did your ancestors come? Do you know about what year they came?
7. Make a list of ten countries from which people came to Pennsylvania. Opposite each give the name of the people, such as: Holland-Dutch, etc.
8. Perhaps some girls who like to sew will want to dress a doll like a Moravian girl.
9. Find out more about the ships that brought people to Pennsylvania hundreds of years ago. Bring pictures to class. Does anyone have a model of a sailing ship?
10. Make paper dolls of a Dutch, Swedish, French, or Amish family. Dress them in the costumes these people wore when they came to Pennsylvania.

PA Historical Commission
Gulielma Penn, first wife of William Penn

## 4. GEORGE WASHINGTON'S DANGEROUS TRIP

### THE ERRAND

"MAJOR WASHINGTON, take this letter to the French leader," said the Governor of Virginia. "You will find him in a fort somewhere near the Ohio River. Wait for a reply to the letter."

"Yes, Sir," said George Washington. At this time, Washington was only twenty-one years old. He was over six feet tall. He had brown hair tied in a short braid, and gray-blue eyes.

"The Frenchmen are trying to take our land away from us," said the Governor. "Your task is to learn what the French plan to do. How many forts do they have? How many Indian tribes will fight for the French? We need to know these things."

"Yes, your Honor," said George Washington. He was proud to be chosen for this dangerous errand.

Washington's horse was waiting for him outside the Governor's mansion. In a few moments, Washington jumped on his horse and rode quickly through the streets of Williamsburg, which was the capital city of Virginia in 1753.

At Fredericksburg, George stopped to say goodbye to his mother. Next he asked a man who could speak French to go with him on the trip. In Alexandria, Washington bought things he would need. In Winchester, he got horses.

Then the two men went on to a village called Wills Creek, which is now Cumberland, Maryland. There Washington went to see a famous scout named Christopher Gist. This man had explored all the land that the King of England had given to the people of Virginia. Washington asked Christopher Gist to be his guide through the forest.

Young George Washington had often camped in the woods. He had made friends with Indians and knew their ways. He could walk as quietly as any Indian, and he was a sure shot with his gun. But he was glad to have Gist as a guide.

It was November 15 when the three men started from Wills Creek. For four days they climbed the mountains. Snow came up to their ankles. It made walking hard.

At the mouth of Turtle Creek, the men came to John Frazier's trading post or store. This store stood near what is now the city of Pittsburgh.

"The French soldiers made me leave my trading post at Venango!" John Frazier told Washington. "They've made my store into a fort! The French soldiers give the

Indians presents. They tell the Indians that the Englishmen will take their land away from them!"

After leaving Frazier's store, Washington and Gist rode horseback over the land that is now Pittsburgh. They saw where two great rivers meet — the Monongahela and the Allegheny. Washington did not know that this spot would one day be called the "Golden Triangle" in the heart of the big city of Pittsburgh! But Washington decided that this spot at the two rivers would be the right place for a fort.

Woodsmen, hired by Washington, brought the canoes and supplies down the Allegheny River. Then the men swam the horses across the stream. Almost at that spot, the Manchester Bridge crosses the Allegheny River today.

The next morning the men reached McKees Rocks. Here lived an Indian named Shingiss. Washington asked Shingiss to go with them.

This land where Washington and the other men walked was dense forest. Today all along the river are many factories. The river is busy with many boats. Washington walked over the land where there are busy towns now.

The men came to a place near what is now called Legionville. Here the French had built a trading post. Here also lived Half King, an Indian chief. Half King, a

Seneca Indian, was a great leader and a friend of the English.

"The French soldiers killed my father!" Half King told Washington. "The French say the land is *theirs*." Old Half King stood straight as a forest tree. "This is *no* white man's land!" he cried. "This is *Indian* land!"

Scotch-Irish Society

The next day a meeting was held in the Indians' longhouse. Washington stood before the Indians. He began to speak:

"Your brother, the Governor of Virginia, has sent me with a letter to the French leader. He tells the Frenchmen to leave this land. My Indian brothers, will you go with me to see the French leader?"

"We will not be friends of the French!" cried Half King. "We will give them back the wampum belt of friendship!"

## THE DANGER

Most of the other Indians did not want the French to be angry with them. Washington waited four days for the Indians to go with him. At last, Washington decided to start through the forest. Only Half King and three other Indians went along.

They went up along Beaver Creek, then turned northeast. At Venango, present-day Franklin, they came to the store which had belonged to John Frazier. Now the store was a fort; over it flew the French flag.

The French captain in charge of the fort greeted

Washington, the other men, and the Indians in a friendly way. He invited them to dinner. The French captain was very friendly to the Indians! He would not take back the wampum belts.

At dinner the French captain said. "We French will never leave this land! Take the Governor's letter to our leader! He will tell you the same thing!"

Washington had to try very hard to be polite. He was angry. He and Gist had trouble getting the Indians to leave the good food and warm house.

At last Washington and the others went on their way. Sometimes they walked through the forest, and sometimes they went by canoe. It rained and it snowed. Finally they reached Fort Le Boeuf.

Major Washington gave the Governor's letter to the man in charge of the fort. His name was St. Pierre. He would not open the letter until the next day. Then another officer came from the French Fort on Lake Erie. The officers had a meeting.

While Washington waited, he and his men counted the canoes and boats at the fort. They counted over two hundred. Washington knew that the French were planning to use the boats to attack in the spring.

During this time the French gave the Indians good things to eat and drink. St. Pierre was an old soldier and sly as a fox. He knew the things the Indians liked best.

He promised the Indians guns. He tried in every way to get the Indians away from Washington.

Finally St. Pierre gave Washington his reply. He said that the land belonged to the French. Then Washington put the letter in his pack, and he and his men started back. The Indians came too. Some of the Frenchmen followed for a while, still trying to get the Indians to stay.

At Venango, Washington decided not to go with the rest of the men. It was cold and snowy. With the horses, travel would be too slow. There was no time to lose. As soon as possible, Washington wanted to warn the Governor of the Frenchmen's plans.

So Washington and Gist started out alone, walking through the forest. An Indian asked to lead them through the woods. Both men soon saw that the Indian was trying to lead them the wrong way! Suddenly, from behind a tree, the Indian fired at them. His shot missed. Before the Indian could fire again, the men took his gun. Gist wanted to kill the Indian, but Washington sent him on alive.

The two men walked all that night and the next day without stopping. They wanted to get away from the Indians who were friends of the French. At last they felt it was safe to get a good sleep.

Washington and Gist planned to cross the Allegheny River on the ice. But the river was not frozen all over.

"We'll have to build a raft," said Washington.

"With one poor hatchet between us!" said Gist.

The two men cut down trees and worked all day. By sunset the raft was finished. The men put the raft in the water and started off. Soon they were halfway across the river.

Suddenly, the raft caught on a big floating cake of ice! Washington was thrown into the cold water! He saved himself by catching hold of the logs. Then he pulled himself up on the raft.

Washington and Gist spent a bitter cold night on an island. Their clothes were stiff with ice. It was such a cold night that the next morning the river was all frozen. The men walked across the ice to the other bank. The Washington Crossing Bridge over the Allegheny River now marks the spot where the men crossed.

Soon Washington and Gist reached John Frazier's store. They were given food and warm clothing. From there they rode to Virginia on horseback.

Again Major Washington stood before the Governor. It was January 16, 1754. "I have St. Pierre's reply, Sir," he said. The letter had stayed safe and dry inside his pack.

# GEORGE WASHINGTON'S DANGEROUS TRIP

Washington had kept a diary of his trip. He had a good report of the land he had seen. He had made a map and he also had a drawing of the French Fort.

The Governor was very much pleased. "The people of the colonies do not know that the French mean to fight," he said. "They do not know that the Indians will help the French. We must let the people know of the danger."

Major Washington's report was printed. It was sent to the leaders in England. The Governor ordered a fort built where the Allegheny and Monongahela rivers meet. The French captured this fort while it was being built. They named it Fort Duquesne. Washington later built a stockade near present-day Uniontown. It was called Fort Necessity.

George Washington became the first leader of the army of the American Colonies that rebelled against British government. He became our first President. Boys and girls in Pennsylvania are proud that young George Washington helped in the making of our state.

52 PENNSYLVANIA PRIMER

## THE ERRAND

### WORDS TO KNOW

| | | |
|---|---|---|
| Allegheny River | major | Pittsburgh |
| Christopher Gist | Monongahela River | Shingiss |
| fort | | task |
| French | Ohio River | Venango |
| guide | | Williamsburg |

### WORD MEANINGS

| | |
|---|---|
| fort | A strong building to defend an area of land. |
| French | The people of France or their language. |
| guide | To lead; one who leads. |
| task | Work to be done. |

## THE DANGER

### WORDS TO KNOW

| | | |
|---|---|---|
| attack | Fort Le Boeuf | polite |
| captain | Fort Necessity | raft |
| diary | | St. Pierre |

### WORD MEANINGS

| | |
|---|---|
| captain | An army officer in command of a company. |

diary      A record written down each day, of thoughts and happenings.

polite      Behaving kindly towards others.

## THINGS TO DO

1. Pretend that you are Major Washington reporting to the Governor.
   a. Make a map to show the land over which you traveled. Mark the route in red.
   b. Write a report. Tell about the French, the Indians, etc.
2. Learn the army ranks—from private to general.
3. Use an encyclopedia to find out more about Fort Duquesne.
4. Mark the French Fort on your big map of Pennsylvania. Show where Fort Necessity was built.
5. On your large outline map, mark the route of Washington's trip through Pennsylvania. Ask your teacher to help you.
6. Washington took with him a man who could speak French. It might be fun to learn some French words.

# 5. THE BATTLE OF BUSHY RUN

IN THE war that followed George Washington's trip to the French fort, there were many battles. The French wanted the land that the English held — land taken from the Indians. The English wanted the land which the French held with their Indian friends.

The Indian allies of the French burned cabins and killed or captured some settlers. The English, on the other hand, kept moving onto lands of the Indians. At last, however, the English were the victors. The Indians did not like this. The Indians who lived near the Great Lakes were afraid that they would be driven from their land by the English. Chief Pontiac led the Indians against the English.

All through Cumberland County to Northampton County, settlers fled from their farms. Important forts were captured by the Indians. Fort Pitt (which had been the French Fort Duquesne), Fort Ligonier, and Fort Bedford still belonged to the English.

It was decided that Colonel Henry Bouquet was to take troops and go to help the men at Fort Pitt. Colonel Bouquet set out from Carlisle on July 18, 1763, with about 500 soldiers. He had a long train of supply wagons

56                                  PENNSYLVANIA PRIMER

PA Historical and Museum Commission
Indians returning captives to Colonel Henry Bouquet and British troops

# THE BATTLE OF BUSHY RUN 57

and pack horses. It took a week to reach Fort Bedford. On August 2, they reached Fort Ligonier. Colonel Bouquet was worried. He had no news from Fort Pitt.

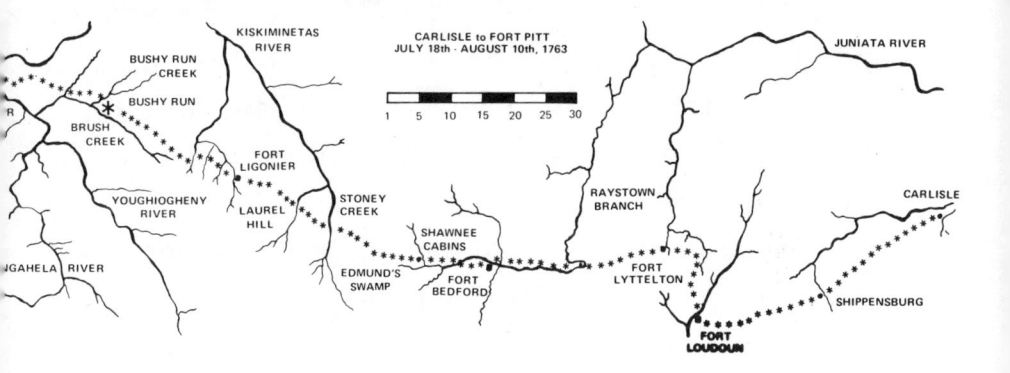

PA Historical and Museum Commission
The westward march of Colonel Henry Bouquet's men

For four days the Indians had been attacking Fort Pitt. There they learned that Colonel Bouquet and his men were on their way to the fort. The Indians decided to leave Fort Pitt and ambush the advance guard of Bouquet's army. To speed up his march, Colonel Bouquet left the wagons and most of his supplies at Fort Ligonier, and went on with his men.

Bouquet's men had rested at Fort Ligonier for two days. Before leaving on August 4, they took the flour from barrels and put it in bags to be carried by the pack horses. The wagons and some of the other supplies were left at Fort Ligonier. Colonel Bouquet planned to march as quickly as possible to Bushy Run. They would enter Turtle Creek valley at dark. In this way he hoped to not be in danger of ambush by the Indians.

A mile away from Bushy Run, however, the advance guard was attacked by Indians. They were fired upon in front and at the rear. There were Indians all around Bouquet's men. The battle lasted from one o'clock in the afternoon until dark. More than sixty of Bouquet's men were killed or wounded. Many horses were killed too.

Bouquet was afraid that no one would live through another Indian attack. That night he gathered his troops on the top of a hill. Flour bags were piled in a circle to form a kind of fort to protect the wounded men.

The next morning the Indians attacked again. They would shoot from one place, disappear, then appear in another place. Bouquet's men were very tired from the long march and the other attack. Also they had no water to drink.

Then Colonel Bouquet thought of a plan. He ordered his men to pretend to retreat. The Indians rushed into the place where the men had been. The very men who had "retreated" fired upon the Indians. Surprised, the Indians were chased back into the forest for two miles.

# THE BATTLE OF BUSHY RUN

Colonel Henry Bouquet

PA Historical Commission

Bouquet's men made litters for the wounded. They destroyed the supplies they could not carry because of the loss of horses. Then they made their way to Fort Pitt. The Indians tried a small attack, but were driven off. Bouquet and his men reached Fort Pitt on August 10. The victory at Bushy Run helped to stop Indian attacks on the settlers.

In 1918 the school children of Westmoreland County gave their pennies to buy six and one half acres of the battlefield site. In 1927 these acres were included in the making of a 162-acre state park. You can visit Bushy Run Battlefield Park today.

## WORDS TO KNOW

| | | |
|---|---|---|
| Chief Pontiac | Fort Ligonier | retreat |
| allies | Colonel Bouquet | litters |
| Fort Pitt | ambush | Cumberland |
| Fort Duquesne | | Northampton |

# THE BATTLE OF BUSHY RUN

## THINGS TO DO

1. On the large Pennsylvania map, show Colonel Bouquet's route from Carlisle to Bushy Run.
2. It took many days for Colonel Bouquet and his men to reach Bushy Run. Use a road map to work out the distance. How long would it take to go by car today?
3. Chief Pontiac was a famous Indian leader. Can you draw his picture?
4. Visit Bushy Run Battlefield.
5. School children once gave money to buy a gift for the state. When was that? What was the gift? Tell all about it.
6. Are pack horses ever used today? Where and why?

## WORD MEANING

ambush    A trap for catching or attacking an enemy by surprise.
allies    Groups or nations that help each other according to the terms of a treaty or agreement.
litter    A stretcher for carrying sick or wounded.
retreat    To withdraw troops from danger or an enemy.

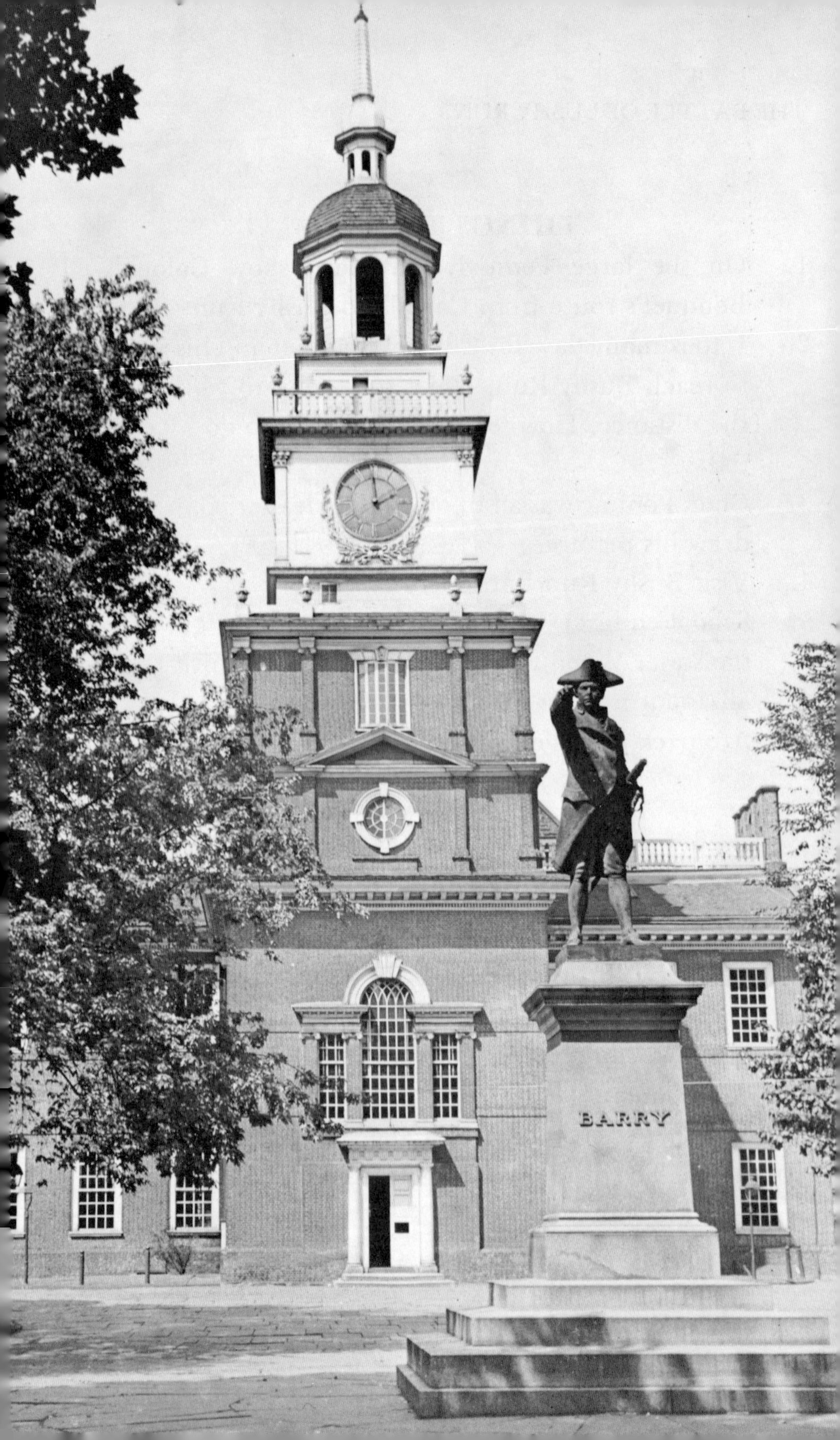
BARRY

## 6.  THE LIBERTY BELL'S STORY

THE PEOPLE of Pennsylvania were proud of their State House, or Capitol. It stood on Chestnut Street in Philadelphia. There the leading men of the province met to talk over the laws. The men also talked over the orders that came from the mother country, England. At that time, Pennsylvania was one of the thirteen colonies in America. The colonies belonged to England.

Some years later a tall tower was added to the red brick State House. A bell was needed for the tower. Soon it would be the year of the 50th birthday of the Charter. The Charter was the plan of government that William Penn had made for Pennsylvania. It was agreed that there should be a State House bell to ring on the Charter's birthday. A bell was ordered to be made in England. The wording to be put on the bell was chosen from a verse in the Bible.

Before long a ship brought the bell to Philadelphia. It was a very handsome, big bell. The bell was hung on a wooden frame in the State House yard. There, before it was raised to the tower, the bell was tried for sound.

PA State Dept. of Commerce

Independence Hall in Philadelphia

Someone sounded the long clapper. The bell rang a few notes. Then there was a dull clank. The big bell had cracked! What a pity.

Should the bell be sent all the way back to England? No, it was decided that two Americans should make the bell over again. The two men chosen were John Pass and Charles Stow, Jr.

When the job was finished, the bell looked good as new. Without a trial ringing, the bell was hung high in the tower of the State House. The workmen who helped to hang the bell were given a big feast.

But when the bell was rung, everyone in the town made fun of its tone! What an ugly voice it had! How the people teased Mr. Pass and Mr. Stow! It was more than the two men could bear. They took the big bell down from the tower and carted it back to their shop. There they broke up the bell, melted the metal, and made it over again. Then, without any party, the bell was hung in the State House. This time, at last, the people were pleased with the sound.

The bell was very busy. It called the leading men of the province to meetings, and called all the people to town meetings. It rang as a fire alarm and as a church bell. It greeted important visitors to the city, and it tolled the deaths of great men.

# THE LIBERTY BELL'S STORY

On July 4, 1776, an important meeting was held in the State House. The men at this meeting had come from all the thirteen colonies of America. Young Thomas Jefferson of Virginia had written a paper called the Declaration of Independence. Should the Declaration be accepted? This meant that the thirteen colonies did not want to belong to England any more. It meant that the colonies wanted to be a new nation. If the men voted to accept the Declaration, there would be war.

It was a hard thing to decide. The men had been talking for several days. At last they voted to accept the Declaration of Independence. No crowd had gathered in the State House yard, but the news soon spread through the town.

Four days later, July 8, the big bell in the State House began to ring. People hurried to the State House yard. All the bells in the city joined in the ringing!

After awhile the bells became quiet. A man stood on a balcony above the State House yard. He read aloud the Declaration of Independence.

After the last word was read, there was a moment's silence. Then the people cheered and cheered! The great bell in the tower rang out again. All afternoon and into the night, the bells of the city rang.

PA Historical and Museum Commission

The Liberty Bell

# THE LIBERTY BELL'S STORY

Every year on the Fourth of July, the State House bell rang to remind the people of the United States of their freedom. One day, however, the bell cracked. It rang its last clear note on Washington's birthday.

Later the bell was taken down from the tower. It was placed on the first floor of the red brick building. Today the Liberty Bell is in a special pavilion on Independence Mall.

When the bell was cast, there wasn't room on the rim for all the words of the Bible verse, and some words were changed. That the bell was made to honor William Penn and his ideas of freedom has long been forgotten. But from the very beginning the bell stood for liberty. And when the colonies declared their freedom, the words held a special meaning:

*"Proclaim liberty throughout all the land unto all the inhabitants thereof."*

## WORDS TO KNOW

| | | |
|---|---|---|
| brick | freedom | Thomas Jefferson |
| charter | greet | tolled |
| clapper | Independence | tone |
| Declaration of | Mall | tower |
| Independence | Liberty Bell | trial |
| feast | | verse |

## WORD MEANINGS

| | |
|---|---|
| brick | A block of clay baked by sun or fire. |
| clapper | Part that strikes a bell. |
| feast | A rich meal made for some special occasion. |
| greet | To say "Hello" or "Welcome." |
| tone | Sound. |

## THINGS TO DO

1. On New Year's Eve, 1975, the Liberty Bell was moved from Independence Hall to a special pavilion on Independence Mall. Plan a visit to this area where there are many historic buildings.
2. With modeling clay make a model of the Liberty Bell.
3. Get a copy of the Declaration of Independence to hang in your classroom.
4. From an encyclopedia find out several more interesting facts about Thomas Jefferson.
5. On the large map of Pennsylvania draw a small Liberty Bell at Philadelphia.
6. Find out from an encyclopedia the name of the first person to sign the Declaration of Independence. Find out the names of Pennsylvanians who signed the Declaration. Who was George Ross? Who was Benjamin Rush?

## 7.  BETSY ROSS AND THE STARS AND STRIPES

WHEN CERTAIN English leaders passed unwise laws to rule the American colonies, some leaders in the colonies believed that they would have to fight for their rights. America had no army. But England had many trained soldiers. So the men and boys in the colonies began to practice to be soldiers. They learned to march and to carry guns as soldiers do.

Now the American soldiers needed a general. Leading men in the colonies met in Philadelphia and voted for a general. George Washington of the colony of Virginia was chosen.

"I don't know if I am wise enough to lead the army," said Washington. "I may make many mistakes. But I will do the best I can for the American Colonies."

Then George Washington rode on horseback to a town near Boston, Massachusetts. There the American soldiers stood in long lines to meet their new general. Under a large elm tree, George Washington took command of the soldiers.

When Washington joined the soldiers, he had a flag. As the flag was raised, thirteen guns boomed! This first flag was called Grand Union. The flag had thirteen red and white stripes. Each stripe stood for one of the thirteen colonies. Where the stars are now located on the flag, the white and red crosses used in the flag of England appeared. This showed that the people of the colonies still felt that America belonged to England.

But the next year the people decided that the colonies should be free from England. On July 4, 1776, you remember, the leading men in the colonies signed the Declaration of Independence.

Now a new flag was needed for a new nation. It is said that Mistress Betsy Ross of Philadelphia made the new flag. She had a small upholstery shop. Betsy's husband, John Ross, had been hurt while guarding ammunition. By accident, some gunpowder exploded. John Ross died from a wound which he received.

George Washington planned the new flag. He made a drawing of his idea. Then he showed the drawing to Mistress Ross.

"The coat of arms of the Washington family is a shield," said George Washington. "On it are three five-pointed stars and three stripes. The shield gave me an idea for a flag."

"The stars in your drawing have six points, General Washington," said Mistress Ross. "I thought you spoke of stars with five points."

"Yes," General Washington replied, "but stars with five points would be hard to cut, wouldn't they?"

"Oh, no," Betsy smiled. She picked up her scissors and a piece of cloth. Then, with one snip of her scissors, she made a five-pointed star!

General Washington was pleased. Mistress Ross promised to have the flag finished by the next day.

When the flag was finished, it was given to General Washington. On June 14, 1777, the leaders of the country voted that the flag Washington had planned was to be the national flag of the United States of America. Today June 14 is known as Flag Day.

This flag was like our flag today, with thirteen red and white stripes. But in the blue field there were only thirteen stars. The stars were in a circle. As the nation grew, stars were added. Each star stands for a state.

The story of Betsy Ross making the first flag is called a legend. No one knows if it is really true, but we like to think it is. It is a known fact that Mistress Ross and the women who helped her made many American flags for the government. Every year, thousands of people visit the small brick house in Philadelphia where Betsy Ross once lived. The house is called "The birthplace of Old Glory."

## WORDS TO KNOW

| Betsy Ross | Grand Union | Old Glory |
| command | legend | practice |
| fact | nation | soldiers |
| general |  | Virginia |

## WORD MEANINGS

fact      Something true or real.

general      A high officer in command of many men in an army.

legend      A story from the past, that many people have believed.

Old Glory      Another name for the flag of the United States.

shield      A piece of armor carried on the arm to protect the body in battle.

## THINGS TO DO

1. Crayon or paint the Grand Union Flag.
2. Crayon or paint the flag Washington planned.
3. Crayon or paint the flag we have now.
4. Ask your teacher to help you cut a five-pointed star.

City of Philadelphia
Betsy Ross' House

5. Learn the song, "There Are Many Flags in Many Lands."
6. Make up a little play about the time General Washington asked Betsy Ross to make the flag. Can you find costumes to wear?
7. In a book, find a picture of the Washington coat of arms.

# 8. A BITTER WINTER AT VALLEY FORGE

ENGLAND SENT well-trained men to fight against the new soldiers of the colonies. Sometimes the Americans won the battles; often they lost.

The English took Philadelphia. After winning a battle on Brandywine Creek in Chester County, English soldiers, in their bright red coats, just marched into the city and made themselves at home. They lived in the finest houses, and they had the best of everything to eat.

During this time General Washington and his men were in the country north of Philadelphia. Washington decided to lead his army to a place called Valley Forge. There, two ridges of land would help to protect the army. Also, there were ways of escape if needed.

It was December 17, 1777, when Washington and his eleven thousand men marched into Valley Forge. They did not really march. No drums or fifes played. The men struggled through the snow. The wind was icy. Not many of the men had uniforms. They wore all kinds of coats and pants. Their shoes were full of holes. Some of the men had no shoes; their feet were wrapped in rags. Others were barefoot.

PA State Dept. of Commerce
Log huts like those used by Washington's soldiers at Valley Forge

The men started small fires to get warm. Those who were strong started to chop down trees and build small log huts. There were not enough tents or blankets for all. General Washington could have gone at once to a warm, nearby house to live. But until some shelter was made for the men, Washington lived in a tent.

There was very little food for the soldiers at Valley Forge. Many of the men became sick and died. Some of the men decided to stop fighting and go home.

Log hospitals were built. A little one-room schoolhouse was used as a hospital. This schoolhouse is still standing. It was built by William Penn's daughter, Letitia, and is probably the oldest schoolhouse in America.

On Christmas Eve, General Washington moved into a small stone house. In February, his wife Martha came from their Virginia home, Mount Vernon, to be with her husband. Mrs. Washington, the wives of officers, and the women of nearby farms were very busy. They spent many hours sewing clothes, patching uniforms, and darning stockings. They made up baskets of food and medicine for the sick soldiers. Martha Washington stayed until the army left Valley Forge in June.

During the terrible winter, General Washington never gave up hope. Washington believed that the American army must not fail to win freedom for the new nation.

# A BITTER WINTER AT VALLEY FORGE

PA State Dept. of Commerce

Washington's headquarters at Valley Forge

His faith cheered the men. Some of the nearby farmers sent wagonloads of food. The country of France promised to send ships, men, and guns to help the Americans.

When spring came, the dogwood burst into bloom all over the hills and dales of Valley Forge. There was hope in the hearts of the men. Now they were certain that the colonies would win their freedom.

The place where Washington and his men camped is now Valley Forge Park. There you can see models of cannon and of the soldier's huts. Some of the houses where the officers stayed are still standing.

You can visit General Washington's stone house. Upstairs you can see Martha Washington's sitting room.

There is a bell tower at Valley Forge. There are fifty-one bells in the tower—one for each state, and a national birthday bell. The bells ring every hour. At sunset the bells play the Star Spangled Banner.

## WORDS TO KNOW

| | | |
|---|---|---|
| dogwood | Mount Vernon | trained |
| fife | ridge | uniforms |
| freedom | shelter | Valley Forge |
| | struggle | |

# A BITTER WINTER AT VALLEY FORGE

## WORD MEANINGS

dogwood — A tree with large white or pink blossoms in the spring, and red berries in the fall.
fife — A small musical instrument played by blowing.
ridge — A long, narrow chain of hills.
struggle — Great effort; hard work.

## THINGS TO DO

1. Can you find pictures of the uniforms of British and American soldiers in the Revolution? If you can, see if you can make crayon copies of them.
2. See if you can find a plan of the American camp at Valley Forge, and then make a wall map of it.
3. You will be interested in finding out more about Martha Washington, especially the months she spent at Valley Forge. Imagine yourself in her place, and write a week's diary about what she did.
4. Mark Valley Forge on the big map. How will you do it?

PA Historical and Museum Commission
David Rittenhouse, an astronomer and government official of colonial Philadelphia.

# PART II

# INTERESTING PEOPLE IN PENNSYLVANIA

Historical Society o
A famous early Pennsylvania gun-maker as portrayed by Benjamin West, an early Pennsylvania a
(Chapter 12)

# 9. A LEGEND ABOUT JOHN HARRIS

WHEN PENNSYLVANIA was a new colony, people settled in and around Philadelphia. As more and more people came, they settled in places farther west of Philadelphia. In 1710, John Harris, who had been born in England in 1673, came to Pennsylvania. He made a living by trading with the Indians. While on a trading trip, he saw the place along the Susquehanna River where he wanted to live. The land in that area was called Pexteng or Paxtang. The Indians told John Harris that he could live there.

First he built a storehouse, and around it a stockade. This was built at what is now the foot of Paxton Street in Harrisburg. Then John Harris built a house. There he lived with his wife, and farmed the land. The Indians brought furs to trade for guns, gunpowder, axes, and other things they wanted. It was a good place for a trading post. At this spot the Susquehanna River was so low that at certain times of the year it was easy to walk or drive a wagon through the water. This was also the place where Indian trails from the east and west met.

John Harris also had a flat ferry boat with which he poled people back and forth across the Susquehanna

River. Many people were going farther west to make homes. They needed a way to get across the river, for there were no bridges. The ferry became very well known. It is said that a letter addressed simply "John Harris, Harris Ferry, North America" reached him.

One day a wandering band of Indians from North Carolina stopped at John Harris's trading post. The Indians had furs to trade, and they wanted rum. Indians had never had rum to drink before the white man came. When they drank the rum, they became drunk. They did not know what they were doing. John Harris saw that these Indians had been drinking. They were noisy and unpleasant.

"Lum! Lum!" the Indians shouted.

"No," said John Harris, "I do not have any rum for you."

"Lum!" the Indians demanded.

"No," said John Harris.

With blood-curdling yells, the Indians grabbed John Harris. They carried him outside and tied him to a mulberry tree on the river bank.

In horror, Hercules, a black servant of John Harris, watched, unseen by the Indians. Then quietly, as the Indians looted the storehouse, Hercules ran to the river. He jumped into a canoe and paddled over to the island where some friendly Indians lived.

# A LEGEND ABOUT JOHN HARRIS

PA Historical and Museum Commission
John Harris stone mansion built at Harrisburg in 1766

John Harris thought his last hour had come. The Indians took all the things they wanted from the storehouse. Then they came back to where he was tied to the mulberry tree. They quickly gathered firewood and piled it against his legs. They laughed at him, holding up jugs of rum. One of the Indians came running with a burning torch. He bent down to set the wood on fire. John Harris closed his eyes, but suddenly he heard a cry.

"Master! Master!"

Another shout was heard, and another! Then John Harris saw the friendly Indians leap upon the others. In terror, the enemy Indians fled. Hercules quickly untied his grateful master.

"Hercules," said John Harris, "when I die, I want to be buried under this mulberry tree."

As he wished, when John Harris died in 1748, he was buried under the mulberry tree. When Hercules died, he was buried at his master's feet. You can see John Harris's grave today on the river bank in Harrisburg.

The son of John Harris, named for his father, was born in 1727. He received grants of land, about eight hundred acres. He continued his father's business of trading and running a ferry. In 1766 he built a big stone mansion. It is now the home of the Dauphin County Historical Society.

# A LEGEND ABOUT JOHN HARRIS

John Harris, Junior, knew that the site where his father had chosen to live would make a fine place for a town. In 1785 the place was called a borough named Harrisburg. In 1812, the state government decided to have offices there. Then in 1819 the cornerstone for the first capitol building was laid.

Long ago this place was a crossroads of Indian trails. Today it is a crossroads for many highways, railroads, and airlines. Harrisburg is the capital of Pennsylvania.

## WORDS TO KNOW

| | | |
|---|---|---|
| borough | historical society | mulberry |
| cornerstone | John Harris | site |
| ferry | legend | stockade |
| grant | looted | storehouse |
| Hercules | mansion | trading post |

## WORD MEANINGS

| | |
|---|---|
| ferry | To carry over a river in a boat. |
| legend | A story from the past that may or may not be true. |
| mansion | A grand house. |
| mulberry | A tree having white or purple berry-like fruit. |
| trading post | A place where goods are exchanged for other goods. Sometimes articles are bought and sold. |

## THINGS TO DO

1. On your outline map draw the mulberry tree at the place on the Susquehanna River where John Harris had his ferry. Beside it draw the capitol dome to show what this place became.
2. If you live in or near Harrisburg, plan a trip to see the grave of John Harris. The stone mansion built by the son of John Harris is a museum now. You would enjoy seeing all the treasures it holds. The museum is near the grave of John Harris.
3. Are there legends told about your part of Pennsylvania?

# A LEGEND ABOUT JOHN HARRIS

4. Harrisburg was named for its founder John Harris. Can you make a list of other places named in the same way?
5. This is the kind of exciting story that is easy to make into a play. Entertain another class with your play.
6. In English class write to the Harrisburg Chamber of Commerce. Ask for information about the Harrisburg of today.
7. Turn the legend about John Harris into an art lesson. Will you use crayon, paint, or cut paper?
8. Make a list of the things you might have seen in the trading post.

## 10. MOLLY PITCHER WITH WASHINGTON'S ARMY

MARY LUDWIG was born in Carlisle, Pennsylvania. When she grew up, she worked as a maid, as did many young girls in those days. Mary worked in the home of William Irvine. Then she met and married John Hays who had a barbershop. Soon after they were married, the Revolutionary War began. The man in whose house Mary had worked became General Irvine. John Hays, Mary's husband, joined the army as a soldier under him. In the winter of 1777-1778, John Hays and General Irvine were in camp at Valley Forge.

Mary went back to work in the Irvine house. All the time, however, she thought about her husband and the men at camp.

"They say that the huts are cold, and there is not enough food for all the men," Mary told Mrs. Irvine. "If only I were there, I could help somehow. I know I could!"

"It's over a hundred miles from here!" said Mrs. Irvine. "How could you ever get there?"

"I will. I know I can do it," said Mary.

Through the snow and bitter cold, it is said Mary rode a horse to Valley Forge. It was a hard trip. She found her husband in the camp, and she helped by cooking, washing, and taking care of the sick.

The Americans were cold and hungry at Valley Forge. But the British army was living in comfort in the city of Philadelphia. The British were warm and well fed all winter. Before dawn on June 18, 1778, the British began to move out of Philadelphia. They crossed the Delaware River, and that evening they camped around Haddonfield, New Jersey.

This news reached General George Washington at Valley Forge before morning. With most of the army, including John Hays' division, General Washington crossed the Delaware River above Trenton. Mary and the other women who had been at Valley Forge went with the army.

On June 28, a hot Sunday, the British and American armies clashed at Monmouth, New Jersey. It was a terrible battle. Mary, seeing men faint in the hot sun, took a pitcher and filled it at a nearby spring. Back and forth, back and forth, she went all day long, bringing water to the thirsty men.

"Molly! Pitcher- Molly—here!" a soldier cried.

"I'm coming," Molly answered.

"Molly! Pitcher!" cried another voice.

PA State Dept. of Commerce
A statue of Molly Pitcher at Carlisle

In this way, Mary Ludwig earned a new name on the battlefield.

Then, suddenly, her husband fell wounded. Quickly, Molly bound the wound with a piece of cloth torn from her petticoat. Then she took John's place. She knew how to load the cannon, and she fired it until the battle ended at nightfall.

The next day the Americans found that the British had fled in the night. Molly was called before General Washington. In front of the troops and her husband, who lay on a cot, General Washington praised Molly for her bravery. Many years later, after her husband had died, the state of Pennsylvania gave Molly money for the rest of her life, because of her help in the Revolutionary War. Monuments in honor of Molly Pitcher can be seen at Carlisle and at the Monmouth Battlefield in New Jersey.

## WORDS TO KNOW

| bravery | General Irvine | monument |
| British | John Hays | Philadelphia |
| cannon | Mary Ludwig | pitcher |
| Carlisle | Monmouth | spring |

## WORD MEANINGS

pitcher     A container for holding and pouring liquids.

spring     A place where water flows or bubbles from the earth.

monument     A building, stone, or statue put up in memory of someone.

## THINGS TO DO

1. If you live near them, go to see the monuments that honor Molly Pitcher—either in Carlisle, Pennsylvania or at the Monmouth Battlefield in New Jersey.
2. In an encyclopedia, read about the cannon used in the Revolutionary War.
3. Molly rode from Carlisle to Valley Forge. Use a road map to see how you can go by car today.
4. We call a woman of courage and daring a heroine. Molly was the heroine of the battle at Monmouth. What other heroines in history have you learned about?
5. See if you can find a poem by an American poet about Molly Pitcher in the library.

6. What was the style of dress worn by women at this time? Dress a doll to look like Molly Pitcher. Perhaps you can make paper dolls of Molly and her soldier-husband John.
7. Make a model of George Washington's headquarters at Valley Forge.
8. You could make a play about Molly Pitcher. You could plan several scenes: at home in Carlisle, Valley Forge, and Monmouth. Imagine the conversations and work out the action.

Benjamin Franklin

## 11. BENJAMIN FRANKLIN AND THE MAKING OF AMERICA

LITTLE BEN FRANKLIN lived in the town of Boston. When he was five years old he could read; at seven he could write. Then his father sent him to school for two years.

When Ben was ten years old, he helped his father who was a candlemaker. In those days everyone needed candles for light. It was a good business. Mr. Franklin hoped that Ben would help him always with the shop.

"I don't want to be a candlemaker," Ben told his father. "I want to be a sailor!"

"That's a foolish notion!" said Mr. Franklin. But if Ben didn't want to be a candlemaker, what would he be? "I know!" Mr. Franklin said one day. "You like to read so much, Ben. Would you like to be a printer?"

"I'd rather be a printer than a candlemaker," Ben replied.

"Good!" Mr. Franklin was pleased. "You can help your brother James in his printing shop."

Ben learned to set type and how to put books together. He liked the work. But he and James quarreled. When Ben was 17 years old, he decided to run away.

Ben took a boat to New York. He didn't find work there, so he traveled on foot to the Delaware River, and then by riverboat to Philadelphia.

When Ben reached the city, he was very tired and hungry. At a bakery he asked for three pennies' worth of bread. To Ben's surprise, the baker gave him three big, puffy rolls!

Ben walked up the street with a roll under each arm, and eating the other. Ben's clothes were untidy from his long journey. His pockets were stuffed with shirts and stockings. He was a funny sight! A girl standing in a doorway laughed at him. But Ben didn't care.

Ben found a printer who needed a helper. He found a room at the same house where the girl had laughed at him! The girl was Deborah Reed. She and Ben soon became good friends.

Some years later Ben became the owner of the little printing shop. When he was 24 years old, he and Deborah were married. Ben printed a newspaper and some books. Before long he had a fine business.

Ben Franklin liked Philadelphia. It was the finest town in America at that time. Ben was always thinking of ways to make Philadelphia an even better place in which to live. He started the first public library. He planned the first hospital in Pennsylvania. He also planned the school which became the University of Pennsylvania.

Ben started the first fire-fighting company in Philadelphia. In those days, men fought fire with buckets of water. Franklin helped to start the first police force and the first city street sweepers in Philadelphia.

Franklin was interested in many things. At that time, men knew there was such a thing as electricity. They did not know much about it, however. Ben wanted to find out if lightning was electricity.

He made a kite and tied a metal key to the lower end of the kite string. One day Ben saw thunderclouds in the sky.

"Billy!" he called to his son. "Hurry!" He and Billy went across the fields to a small shed.

"Now, Billy, raise the kite!" Ben cried. Then, at the right moment, he touched the doorkey. There was a bright spark. Ben felt the sting of electricity!

Soon after this Ben invented the lightning rod. It saved many houses from being burned. In those days, a fireplace was the only way to heat a room. Ben invented the Franklin stove; it gave better heat than a fireplace. He invented a rocking chair and many other things.

Franklin also improved mail delivery. In early days the mail was carried by a man on horseback. Then it was carried by stage coach. When our nation, the United States, was formed, Benjamin Franklin was in charge of

Rare Book Dept. of the Free Library of Phila.
A view of Franklin's Philadelphia

the mail.

Franklin was now a great leader in America. He was sent first to England and then to France on important missions for the thirteen colonies. He made many friends for his country.

Franklin was invited to visit the King of France. He did not wear a fancy wig or carry a cane, as was the style. He wore a simple brown velvet suit. The King and all the people were pleased with old Dr. Franklin.

When Franklin returned to America, he helped to plan the laws for the new nation, the United States. Along with men like George Washington and Thomas Jefferson, he helped to found a new nation.

## WORDS TO KNOW

| Benjamin Franklin | colonies | New York |
|---|---|---|
| Boston | Deborah Reed | notion |
| business | electricity | police |
| candlemaker | hospital | type |
|  | library | university |
|  | lightning rod |  |

## WORD MEANINGS

library     A collection of books or the place where the books are kept.
notion     Idea.
police     Men who work for government to keep order.

## THINGS TO DO

1. Benjamin Franklin was fond of writing wise sayings which have become famous. "Early to bed and early to rise, makes a man healthy, wealthy and wise," is one of them. Can you find three others?
2. It will be a surprise to find out how many brothers and sisters Ben had.
3. Learn exactly how a lightning rod works.
4. From your school library get another book or short story about Franklin. Report to your class new things you learn about him.
5. Appoint a committee from your room to plan a visit to a print shop or publishing house.
6. At a class meeting make suggestions about how to represent Franklin on your big map. Vote to decide.
7. Find out how candles were made by hand.

## 12. BENJAMIN WEST, THE BOY WHO LIKED TO PAINT PICTURES

"THERE!" BENNY WEST set the three small boards against the fence. "Now I have something to paint on!" Benny was a Quaker boy who lived in Pennsylvania many years ago. He was just seven years old. More than anything else, Benny liked to draw pictures. But he had no pencils, paper, or brushes to use. He had never seen a picture made by anyone else!

Benny ran into the barn to the little cupboard which held his painting things. There was red and white chalk and pieces of soft yellow stone. There were two pouches of red and yellow clay that the Indian squaw had given to him. The clay mixed with lard would make real paint; the Indians mixed the clay with bear's grease to paint their faces. There was a bluing stick Benny had begged from his mother. Mrs. West used the bluing stick to whiten washed clothes; Benny would use it for blue paint.

"Red, yellow, and blue I have!" Benny sang. He picked up the goose and chicken feathers he used for brushes. Then he picked up a small stump of wood with a patch of cloth tied over the end; this too was a brush.

Suddenly something rubbed against Benny's legs. Benny jumped. "Puss!" he cried, "Thee frightened me."

The black cat purred loudly, begging to be petted.

Benny squatted down beside her. "Did thee catch any mice today?" he asked. He stroked the cat's silky head, her smooth back, and beautiful, long tail.

All at once, Benny had a wonderful idea! "Thee dear pussy!" he cried.

"Puss! Puss!" Benny coaxed the cat across the yard and into the kitchen. No one was there. Benny could hear his mother talking with his older sister in the next room.

Benny poured some rich milk into a saucer. Then, holding the saucer in one hand, he opened the drawer of the kitchen table with the other. Yes, there was a pair of scissors! Carefully, carefully, so that it would not squeak, Benny closed the drawer.

Then Benny set the dish of milk on the floor. "It's for thee!" he told the cat. The black cat lapped the milk, purring with delight. Benny stroked her gently. Then he took the scissors.

"I won't hurt thee!" Benny promised the cat.

"Snip-snip!" went the scissors. There in Benny's hand lay the long black hair which had been the very tip of the cat's tail!

"Now I will have a fine brush!" Benny said. "Thank thee, pussy!"

Benny took a piece of string from his pocket and tied the hair together. "Now I need a handle for my brush," he said. Again he looked in the table drawer.

Just then the door into the other room opened. "Oh, it's thee, Benny," said his mother. "Did thee have a good day at school?"

"Yes," Benny replied, quickly closing the drawer. He put the tuft of cat's hair into his pocket.

Mrs. West saw the cat and the empty dish, but she only said, "Sister and I would like to gather flowers in the garden. Benny's here, Sister," she called. "He will mind the baby."

Benny's married sister was home for a visit. She laid her little Sally into the cradle. All ten West children had slept in that wooden cradle.

"Here," said Sister, giving Benny a fan to shoo the flies. Then she and Mrs. West went into the garden.

Benny sighed with disappointment. He wanted to try his cat's hair brush, paints, and boards right away! Scowling, Benny sat down beside the cradle.

Benny's eyes were always busy. As he looked around the room, he made a picture of the room in his mind. He sighed again, then looked at the sleeping baby.

He seemed really to see her for the first time. He saw her round head, long lashes, baby mouth, and button nose. "I could paint Sally!" Benny thought. Then he saw the ink, black and red, on the table. There was a quill pen and paper, too.

"I'll draw Sally with ink!" Benny said. In a few minutes he was busy drawing. Benny forgot that Quakers did not think it right to make a likeness of a person. He forgot about everything but the joy of drawing.

All at once Benny heard someone behind him. He tried to hide the paper.

"Mother!" Sister held up the drawing. "See what Benny has done!"

Mrs. West laid down the flowers she had gathered, and looked at the drawing. She did not scold. Somehow she knew that her youngest son had been given a special gift. She put her arms around Benny. "Thee has made a good likeness of dear little Sally!" she said.

As Benny grew older, he had to help his father. Benny's home was also an inn where travelers stopped to eat and stay the night. But Benny always found time to draw. One day a cousin sent him a box of real oil paints! An artist in Philadelphia gave him books about painting to study.

When Benny was twelve years old, he began to earn money painting pictures of people. These pictures were called portraits. One time his father went with him to Lancaster, so that Benny could make portraits. He became known for miles around as a portrait painter.

The Quaker friends of the West family agreed that Benny had a special talent. So Benny went to Philadelphia to study art. Later he traveled in Europe. King George III of England liked the Quaker, Benjamin West, and his work, very much. Benjamin was made Court Painter! That is, he painted pictures for the King. All during the War of Independence, when the Americans were fighting against Mother England, King George and Benjamin West were friends.

Benjamin West became very famous. He became the friend and teacher of American artists even more famous than he. The house where he lived as a boy is still standing on the grounds of Swarthmore College in Swarthmore, Pennsylvania.

### WORDS TO KNOW

| brushes | feathers | quill |
| chalk | paints | silky |
| cradle | portrait | scold |
| disappointment | pouch | scissors |

## WORD MEANINGS

| | |
|---|---|
| cradle | A baby's little bed on rockers. |
| portrait | A picture of a person. |
| pouch | A bag or sack. |
| quill | A large stiff feather, sometimes made into a pen. |

## THINGS TO DO

1. Can you paint a picture using a chicken feather or a stick covered with cloth for a brush?
2. Look for copies of some of Benjamin West's portraits.
3. Write a short poem about the boy Benny West, or a poem about the black cat.
4. It would be fun to have an art lesson on portraits. Bring some copies of portraits to class. Your teacher can give you some hints about how to draw the head, place the eyes, etc. Or perhaps there is a book in your library about easy ways to draw heads. Try to draw a classmate. You will be surprised to find how good the portrait will be.
5. Do you know how to mix colors using only red, yellow, and blue paint?

# 13. JAMES FORTEN, BLACK SAILMAKER EXTRAORDINARY

Y EARS AGO ships did not have motors. They had sails made of canvas. Wind made the ships move. In Philadelphia, Mr. Robert Bridges owned a sail loft where strong sails were made. There were forty sailmakers in the loft. Some were blacks.

One day Mr. Bridges stopped to speak to a young black boy who was helping his father. "You work well, James," he said with a smile. Then he spoke to the boy's father, Thomas Forten, a sailmaker. "He's a good lad."

Mr. Forten, busy sewing rope to the edge of a sail, nodded his head in agreement. Mr. Forten was a free black because his father, born into slavery, had earned enough money outside of slave hours, to buy his freedom.

"I like to work," nine-year-old James said with a grin. He often helped and earned an extra shilling. He threaded needles with twine for the sailmakers, or rubbed the twine with a ball of wax.

James lived with his father, mother, and sister, Abigail, in a small wooden house near the Delaware River. He went to a school for black boys and girls. It was taught by Anthony Benezet, a Quaker. Outside of school, James' favorite game was playing marbles.

One day, however, James' father fell from a boat into the river and died. James never went to school again. He had to find work so that he could take care of his mother and sister. James wanted to work in the sail loft, but he was too young. Instead, he got a job as a helper to a chimney sweep.

In those days, every home was heated by a wood fire in a fireplace. The fireplace chimneys had to be kept clean. The man who did this was called a chimney sweep. James' job was to climb up inside the chimney and brush away the soot. He did not like this dirty job.

Then Mr. Benezet helped him to get a job in a grocery store. James swept the store and kept the place tidy. He also delivered groceries. He liked this job, but he didn't earn much money.

When James was eleven years old, the American colonies declared their independence from England. All his life, James remembered the day the Declaration of Independence was read aloud at the State House. The bells in the city rang all day and into the night. Bonfires were burned to celebrate.

When the Revolutionary War began, however, there were many hardships. American money was worth very little. With it, people could not buy what they needed. James was now fourteen, tall, and strong. He begged his mother to let him get a job on a ship.

"I'm afraid that you would be captured!" said his mother. Both mother and son knew that a captured black sailor was often sold as a slave.

But James needed the money. He got a job as a powder boy on the *Royal Louis*. It was a new American ship that would hunt for British ships. James' job was to carry powder from the storeroom to the gunners.

The *Royal Louis* won several victories. But before long, it was captured by a British warship. Sir John Beasly was the captain of the British ship. When the captured crew went aboard the warship, Sir John saw that James carried a small bag of marbles. He sent his son William, who was on the ship, to ask James to play a game. The boys became friends and spent many hours playing marbles.

William Beasly, who was near James' age, asked his father if they could take James to England with them.

"You will have a home with us, and you will be sent to fine schools." said Sir John.

James hesitated. What a wonderful life it would be! At last, he slowly answered. "Thank you, sir, but I cannot. I would be a traitor to my country."

So James, with the rest of the captured crew, was taken to the prison ship *Jersey*, which was moored in the East River near New York City. The *Jersey* was a dreadful place. The prisoners were kept in the hold of the ship. It was dark and airless. During the day, prisoners were allowed on deck, but many were sick. All were covered with lice. The food was not fit to eat. The water was not clean.

James was filled with horror. He offered to help wash the decks, to do other chores, and to help with the sick. In the days that followed, James stayed well. He saw, however, that his friend Daniel Brewton, who also had been a powder boy, looked ill. Daniel's face was pasty white; he was very thin.

James made many friends among the prisoners. One of these was an officer who was soon to be released.

"Will you help me carry my sea chest to the boat in the morning?" he asked young James. The boy looked at the large chest.

"I could hide in it!" he whispered to the officer. The officer nodded. Then James remembered Daniel— Daniel who would soon die if he stayed on the ship.

The next day James helped to carry the sea chest. In it was Daniel. The white boy lived to be an old man, and over and over again he told how James Forten had saved his life.

James was a prisoner for seven months. When freed, his clothes were in tatters. He walked barefoot all the way home to Philadelphia. His mother and sister cried with joy when they saw him.

When James was seventeen years old, he wanted to go to England. His sister's husband was a sailor. James and his brother-in-law were hired as seamen on the same ship. When James reached England, he found work on the docks. He helped to load and unload ships. He also heard true stories about how slaves were treated. He went to meetings where white men spoke against slavery. James was thankful that he was a free man. He felt great pity for black slaves.

When James went back to the United States, he became an apprentice to Robert Bridges, the sailmaker. In two years, twenty-two year old James Forten became foreman of the sail loft. He learned quickly. From a drawing, James now could make a sail ready to be fastened to the mast of a ship.

In 1793 a terrible disease called yellow fever swept over Philadelphia. Five thousand people died. James was among the many black people who helped nurse white people. He also helped to bury the dead.

James married the next year, but his young wife died. His sister's husband had been lost at sea. James took care of his sister, her two children and his mother. Later he married a girl named Charlotte. They lived in a handsome, three-story brick house on Lombard Street. In time they had eight children.

In 1798, Mr. Bridges planned to retire. He wanted James to buy the business, but James did not have enough money. And who would lend a black money? Then James remembered how Mr. Willing, the wealthy shipper, had given him books to read and had encouraged him to read and write. Mr. Willing owned the warehouse that held the sail loft. Also Mr. Willing had admired the device that James had invented to handle sails. "I'll ask Mr. Willing," James decided.

Mr. Willing talked it over with Mr. Bridges. He then agreed to lend the money to James. In return, James was to outfit all Willing ships with his invention.

In the years that followed, James had the best sail loft in Philadelphia, and made a fortune. Much of the money, however, he gave away to help others. He did all he could to help stop slavery and to better the lives of free blacks. He attended anti-slavery meetings. He gave money so that slaves could buy their freedom. He wrote articles to plead for the rights of blacks. He helped to enlist black soldiers to help in the War of 1812 against England. Later he helped slaves to escape from their southern masters. He talked against the starting of a black colony in Africa. His home was in Philadelphia and he did not want to leave it. He believed that other blacks felt the same way.

James Forten lived to be seventy-five years old. At his death, thousands of people came to his funeral—and half of them were white. He was admired and respected by all.

## WORDS TO KNOW

| | | |
|---|---|---|
| Abigail | Declaration of | James Forten |
| Anthony Benezet | Independence | Robert Bridges |
| canvas | delivered | sailmaker |

## WORD MEANINGS

anti-slavery  Against slavery.
article  A written composition that is part of a magazine, book, or newspaper.
device  A mechanical invention used for a special purpose.
encourage  To give hope, courage, or confidence; to urge on.
hardship  Something hard to bear. Hunger, cold, and sickness are hardships.
mast  A long pole of wood or steel set up on a ship to hold the sails and rigging.

moor        To put or to keep a ship in place by means of ropes or chains fastened to the shore or to anchors.
shilling    A British silver coin. In earlier days it was worth about 24 cents in United States money.
shipper     One who ships goods to other areas.
traitor     A person who betrays a friend, a duty, his country, etc.
warehouse   A place where goods are kept.

## THINGS TO DO

1. Can you make a model of a ship with sails? Look up in a book the kind of sailing ship that was used in 1776.
2. Can you draw a picture of a sailing ship?
3. Find out the names of sails and rigging.
4. Write down the reasons why James Forten was admired and respected by all people.

## 14.  LUCRETIA MOTT

"HERE'S SOMETHING to eat," Lucretia whispered. She slipped a piece of buttered bread under the door of the closet. Inside was a boy who had broken a rule at school. He was to spend the day in the closet with only dry bread to eat and some water to drink. Lucretia, however, thought this was unfair. Even at thirteen, lively, dark-haired Lucretia did what she thought was right.

Lucretia liked boarding school. In those days before the Civil War, few girls were sent to school. Lucretia's mother and father believed that girls as well as boys should go to school.

While at this Quaker school in New York State, Lucretia often saw black slaves. They worked on farms nearby. Lucretia began to think that slavery was wrong.

Lucretia's best friend was Sarah Mott. At vacation time, Lucretia went home with Sarah. Lucretia liked Sarah's brother James, too. He was tall, sandy-haired and quiet.

When Lucretia was sixteen, she was made a teacher. At the end of the term, however, Lucretia wanted to go home to Boston. She had been away from her family for three long years.

Later, Lucretia's family moved to Philadelphia. Her father gave James Mott a job in his store. After six months, James became a partner in the business. Soon after this, Lucretia and James were married.

There were good times and bad times for the Motts. Six children were born to them. Lucretia was kept busy with her large family. She was interested in more than just keeping house, however. She liked to know about what was happening in the world. Once she surprised even herself and spoke out in a Friends Meeting. Later, she became a preacher of the Society of Friends. Lucretia wanted to help make the world a better place in which to live.

Lucretia often thought about the black slaves. She bought only sugar and rice grown without the help of slaves. James now owned his own store. He sold cotton, but not cotton grown by slave-holders in the South. He could not get enough of this cloth, however. He had to earn a living for his family, so at last he was forced to sell cotton cloth made from cotton picked by slaves. Later, however, he went into the wool business.

James belonged to a society to do away with slavery. Benjamin Franklin had started this anti-slavery society. The people who belonged to the society hoped to free the slaves over a number of years. Then some thought the slaves could be sent back to Africa.

One day, Lucretia was asked to speak in a black church. After the service, James Forten, a black leader, talked with her.

"I was born in Philadelphia," he said. "I grew up here. Should I be sent to Africa to live in a hut as my forefathers did?"

Lucretia saw that this was a foolish idea. Black and white people must learn to live together here in the United States.

In 1833 sixty men came to Philadelphia to hold the first anti-slavery convention. They invited women to come to the meeting. Lucretia went and even jumped to her feet to speak. Outside of Friends Meetings, women never spoke in public. Everyone stared at her. But what she said was helpful. The very next week she started an anti-slavery society for women. She also started an anti-slavery sewing society. The women met every week. They made aprons, pincushions, and cloth bags (used like pocketbooks) to sell at an anti-slavery fair. The society also started a school for black children with a black teacher to run it.

In those days most of the people of Philadelphia were not against slavery. And so the anti-slavery women could not rent a hall to have a convention. People in favor of free speech raised money to build a hall of their own. They called it Pennsylvania Hall. It was to be opened on

May 14, 1838. Anti-slavery people from all over the North came to Philadelphia. The Motts took fourteen people into their home, including two black women.

Signs against the convention were put up in the city. A mob gathered outside the hall. The police said they could not do anything about the mob. The speakers in the hall tried not to pay any attention to the noise of the mob — or to the bricks thrown through the windows. Lucretia Mott had just finished speaking when a cry was heard: "Fire!"

Smoke poured into the first floor. Boys and men with axes and blazing torches broke into the building. The women escaped out a side door. The mob built a bonfire in the hall. When the firemen came, they did nothing to stop the fire. They only poured water on buildings next door.

The next day the anti-slavery women walked through the streets to a little schoolhouse. People jeered at them, but they held their meeting. They decided and wrote down on paper that they would sit with blacks in church, visit them in their homes, and treat them in every way the same as white people. This was a new idea at that time.

All that day mobs roamed the streets. In the evening, Lucretia and James expected the mob to burn their house. They sent their young children away and took

The burning of Pennsylvania Hall by a mob in 1838

clothing and some furniture to a friend's house. Some Quaker friends stood by the Motts. Suddenly fifteen-year-old Tom Mott came running.

"They're coming!" he shouted. Lucretia took her husband's hand. She could hear the noise coming closer. But then, the noise grew fainter. Aferwards, the Motts learned that a friend had led the mob the wrong way. Shouting, "On to the Motts!" he led them on up Race Street instead of turning into Ninth. That night the mob tried to burn an orphans' home for black children, and the offices of a newspaper in favor of Pennsylvania Hall.

Lucretia continued to go to meetings and to do what she could to help the blacks. In those days there were no buses. Cars were pulled by horses. Every fifth car was for blacks. If a black got on another car, he had to stand on an outside platform. One stormy day Lucretia was on a car when a sickly black woman entered. The conductor told the woman to stand outside.

"Won't you please let her come inside?" asked Lucretia.

"It's the rule," said the conductor.

So Lucretia went out and stood beside the black woman in the rain. Lucretia was then an old lady. The conductor asked her to come in out of the rain.

"I cannot, without this woman," she replied.

"Oh, well, bring her in then," said the conductor.

Soon afterwards an order allowed the blacks to ride inside on any of the cars.

Lucretia worked all her life to better the lives of blacks. She was glad when the slaves were freed at last. But there was still much to be done to help the freed blacks. Lucretia lived to be eighty-seven years old. When she died, more than a thousand people came to her funeral. When someone asked, "Will no one speak?" another answered, "The preacher is dead."

Lucretia Mott believed that every black should have the chance to be a free American citizen, with the same rights as others. Her work to help those in need was a good example to others—then and now.

## WORDS TO KNOW

anti-slavery society    boarding school    convention
Boston

## WORD MEANINGS

| | |
|---|---|
| anti-slavery society | A group of persons united against slavery. |
| convention | A meeting arranged for a particular purpose. |
| mob | A lawless crowd, easily moved to act without thinking. |

## THINGS TO DO

1. You may all like to learn more about Lucretia Mott. She was born in 1793 on Nantucket Island, Massachusetts. Her father was a sea captain. She learned to knit, weave, and make candles. She loved the moors, the cobblestone streets, and the cranberry bogs of her island home. Nantucket Island is a well-known place to visit today. Can you find a book about it in your library? Do you knit or weave? Can you make a candle? Look up in a book how candles used to be made.

2. When Lucretia lived, ladies almost never made speeches, but Lucretia did! Write a speech such as she might have made against slavery. Read it to the class.

3. Lucretia's father was the captain of a sailing ship. He sailed to China and to India. Look up in a book the kind of ship in which he would have sailed at that time. Memorize a sea chant like those his sailors may have sung. "Blow the Man Down" is a good one.
4. Find a picture of Lucretia Mott in a book. Notice her Quaker bonnet and plain dress. Can you draw her?
5. Is there a Society of Friends' meetinghouse near where you live? Can you tell your class about a Friend's meeting?
6. Make a list of men and women who have helped to better the lives of black people.

## 15.      JOHN JAMES AUDUBON, PAINTER OF BIRDS AND ANIMALS

"LOOK! look, Mama!" little John James called. He opened the small basket that had held his lunch. In the basket were a bird's nest, some feathers, a few wilted flowers, and a tiny blue egg!

"All day you have spent in the woods!" Mama pretended to scold. "What would your father say!"

John James put both arms around his mother and hugged her tight. "Learning in the woods is better than learning from books!" he said. "The little birds were hatched and gone from the nest, or I would not have taken it!"

Mama loved this fine boy who was not her own child. His real mother was dead. Mama loved Rosa, his sister, too.

The children's father was an officer in the French Navy. He was not at home very often. Captain Audubon hoped that his son also would be a seaman.

One day when John James was about fourteen years old, Captain Audubon came home from a sea trip. After dinner, Rosa played the piano for him. Very much pleased, Captain Audubon gave his daughter a book.

"Now, my son," he said to John James, "play something for us on your violin."

"The strings of my violin are broken, Father," John James replied. "I have not played the violin for a long time. I am sorry."

"Well, it doesn't matter," Captain Audubon said, "Have you any drawings to show me?"

John James brought his father a few drawings. Alas, his work was no better. John James had spend most of his time just playing idly in the woods.

Captain Audubon did not scold. But early the next morning he took his son on a trip. He took him to the place where he was staying. Now Captain Audubon could watch over his son. This was a good lesson for the boy. Captain Audubon soon saw, however, that his son never would make a seaman.

Before long, Captain Audubon took John James back home. He sent the boy to school there. One year he sent John James to Paris where the boy was taught drawing by a famous painter. But John James wasn't happy. He wanted to draw nothing but birds and animals. Already he had made two hundred drawings of birds!

Captain Audubon owned land in the United States. "Someone should look after my place there," he said. "It is called Mill Grove, and it is not far from Philadelphia."

John James had heard often of the wild forest in America. He wanted to see the strange birds and flowers. "Father," he asked, "May I go to Mill Grove?"

Captain Audubon was pleased that his son was willing to go to a strange country alone. "We will begin to plan at once!" he told John James.

In 1803, young Audubon started for America. When John James reached the United States, he was ill. Quaker friends took care of him. When he was well, Audubon went to his father's place, Mill Grove. Will Thomas and his wife, who took care of the house, warmly welcomed the young man.

Audubon liked the house and land. Mill Grove stood on a hill above Valley Forge. A little path led to the old mill on the Perkiomen Creek. The woods near the house was filled with birds and flowers.

Mr. and Mrs. Thomas did everything to make young Audubon happy. All the neighbors liked this charming young Frenchman. Audubon with his long, curly hair, satin coat and breeches, and shiny patent leather shoes soon was well-known in the countryside around Mill Grove. John James was happy drawing birds, hunting, fishing, and going to parties. He fell in love with Lucy Bakewell, a neighbor's daughter.

# JOHN JAMES AUDUBON

For a while, Audubon took a job in New York City. He wanted to earn enough money so that he could marry Lucy and take care of her. But the job did not interest him. He wanted only to draw birds.

Then Audubon and a friend decided to open a store in the western part of the United States. Audubon, now twenty-three years old, came back to Pennsylvania. He married Lucy Bakewell and took her with him.

Audubon and Lucy went to Pittsburgh—250 miles away—by stagecoach over rough roads. From there they went down the Ohio River on an open flatboat steered by oarsmen. They had a long, happy trip.

When they reached Louisville, Kentucky, they liked the town and the people. Here Audubon and his friend had their store. But Audubon did not make a good storekeeper. His business failed.

Then Audubon earned money by drawing pictures of people in colored crayons. Later, he moved Lucy and their two boys to Ohio. Audubon took a job in a museum. Also, he and Lucy opened a school.

"Lucy," Audubon said one day, "I want to paint all the birds in America!"

"Then you shall!" agreed his wife. "I'll stay here to teach and take care of the boys."

This is what Lucy did. Audubon wandered far and wide over the country, drawing birds. He made hundreds of pictures. He also wrote down everything he could learn about how birds build their nests and how they live.

Then Audubon decided to go to England to have his pictures of birds printed. At that time no one in America could do the printing as he wanted. On the trip to England Audubon made drawings of the birds of the ocean.

In England, Audubon was called a great American artist. People paid high prices for his paintings. Many people wanted to buy the book he planned to have printed, *Birds of America*. The book cost hundreds of dollars!

Audubon was given many honors for his work. He began at once to make more pictures for other books.

When Audubon was almost sixty years old, he took another long trip. He went through the forest of northwestern United States. He drew pictures and wrote about the birds and animals that he saw.

The last years of his life, Audubon spent with his family. They lived in a house close to New York City. The woods near the house was filled with birds. Many animals—elk, moose, bear, and foxes—were kept in large pens near the little building called "the painting house." Audubon, Lucy, their children and grandchildren were very happy here. Audubon grew old in years, but he was always young in heart. This house and land are called Audubon park in New York City. It is a place bird lovers like to visit.

Mill Grove, the house near Valley Forge, is also open to everyone. It is at Wetherill Corners, just three miles from Washington's house in Valley Forge Park.

Audubon had many friends. Today he has many more friends. The Audubon Society, named in his honor, has many thousands of members—men, women, boys and girls—who love, study, and protect birds. Maybe you would like to belong to the Junior Audubon Society.

When you listen to the song of the woodthrush or watch a frisky squirrel, perhaps you, too, will remember John James Audubon who loved all wild creatures. Perhaps, too, you will remember the story of the happy times Audubon spent with Lucy Bakewell at Mill Grove, Pennsylvania.

## WORDS TO KNOW

| | | |
|---|---|---|
| breeches | Lucy Bakewell | Perkiomen Creek |
| creature | military | storekeeper |
| John James | Mill Grove | violin |
| Audubon | museum | wander |
| | Paris | |

## WORD MEANINGS

breeches    Short trousers fastened below the knees.
creature    Any living person or animal.
wander    To move about without any special plan.

## THINGS TO DO

1. Choose a bird that lives all or part of the year in Pennsylvania. On a large sheet of drawing paper, draw, then color or paint your bird. Below, tell all about the nest, eggs, food, habits, etc. of the bird. Display the birds on your bulletin board.
2. Select a wild animal that lives in Pennsylvania. Make a picture of it. Below the drawing, write carefully about its home, food, habits, etc. Show the pictures on your bulletin board.

3. Your class can have a junior Audubon Club. It is a wonderful way to learn about birds and wildlife. For a few cents, the Audubon Society will send manuals, pamphlets, teaching ideas, and all sorts of things for young people to do. Write to:
   The National Audubon Society
   950 Third Avenue
   New York, New York 10022

4. It is easy to build a bird feeding station. You might wish to have one on a window sill of your classroom or your bedroom at home. Supply it with bird seed, suet, raisins, and peanut butter. Keep a record of the bird visitors.

5. Plan a nature corner in your classroom. Show there any pictures, stories, plants, flowers or animals that classmates can bring to school.

6. Does your library in school, or another nearby library, have a copy of Audubon's book *Birds of America?* Bring it to class.

7. Make a decorative mobile of birds to hang in your classroom. These birds need not be life-like; they can be designs. Perhaps you would like to make the birds by folding paper in the Japanese manner. Two books to help you are:

Massoglia, Elinor T. *Fun-Time Paper Folding,* (Children's Press 1959).

Hondo, Isao. *How to Make Origami,* (McDowell 1959).

The National Gallery of Art
Audubon's "Columbia Jay"

## 16.  STEPHEN GIRARD, RICHEST MAN IN AMERICA

STEPHEN GIRARD was born in France. His father was a sea captain. Because of an accident, Stephen lost the sight of one eye. When he was fourteen years old, he left home to be a cabin boy on a ship.

For ten years Stephen was a sailor. Then he became captain of an American merchant ship — a ship that carried goods to different countries. One night in the spring of 1776 Girard's ship was caught in a bad storm. He put down the anchor. In the morning there was such a thick fog, no one could tell where the ship was.

As a signal for help, Girard fired a cannon. A pilot boat soon appeared out of the fog.

"Where are we?" Girard called.

"You are in Delaware Bay," the pilot told him.

"I want to go to New York," said Girard.

"You can't," answered the pilot. "The United States is at war with England. The English ships will capture you. You've escaped because of the fog. You'd better sail up to Philadelphia."

So, in this way, Girard happened to come to Philadelphia. He stayed and made the city his home. In a few years Girard owned several ships. He was a good business man. He soon owned a whole fleet of ships.

Girard was not very kind to anyone who worked for him. He never gave money to beggars, but he did give to churches and to the poor. He was a hard man to understand. Yet he was good to his relatives, kind to his pets, and well-loved by children.

In the summer of 1793 a very serious disease called yellow fever swept through Philadelphia. At that time no one knew that yellow fever was spread by mosquitoes. Everyone was afraid of the terrible illness. Stephen Girard wasn't afraid. He went to a hospital and helped to nurse the sick people. He also used his own carriage to bring the sick to the hospital.

In 1812 England took sailors from American ships to help in England's fight against France. The United States had to declare war on England. None of the rich men wanted to lend money to the United States government. But Stephen Girard did. It was Girard's money that bought supplies and helped to win the War of 1812.

When Girard was eighty-one years old, he was the richest man in the United States. He never stopped working, however.

Girard knew that he could not live much longer. He asked some lawyers to help him decide what to do with his millions of dollars. Girard gave much money to help

Courtesy of Girard College

Modern-day orphan students in front of the "college" built by Stephen Girard

other people. He gave money to the public schools in Philadelphia. Then he told the lawyers of this plan:

"The rest of my money is to be used to build and keep a school. It is to be called Girard College. Only boys who have lost a parent will come to this school. When the boys enter the school, they must be between the ages of six and ten years. They will learn to be obedient and good workers. They may stay until they are eighteen and have learned how to earn a living."

The lawyers did as Girard wished. More than a hundred years have passed since Girard died. More than thirteen thousand boys have graduated from the Girard school in Philadelphia! These boys were taught to earn a living. They grew up to be mechanics, carpenters, lawyers, doctors, ministers, and many other kinds of workers.

The walled school grounds are now surrounded by an almost all black section of the city. A long legal battle was fought to change Girard's will so that black as well as white orphan boys could enter the school. Finally, in May 1968, the trustees of the school agreed to admit black boys.

## WORDS TO KNOW

| | | |
|---|---|---|
| accident | citizen | mechanics |
| anchor | declare | merchants |
| captain | doctors | millions |
| carpenter | fleet | mosquitoes |
| carriage | | Stephen Girard |

## WORD MEANINGS

| | |
|---|---|
| captain | Commander of a ship. |
| carpenter | Worker who builds with wood. |
| declare | Say. |
| fleet | A group of ships under one command. |

## THINGS TO DO

1. Is there a boy or man in your town who has gone to Girard College? Ask him to give a talk to your class about his school.
2. A committee of children interested in science could find out all they can about yellow fever and tell the class what they have learned.

## 17.  STEPHEN FOSTER, AND HIS SONGS THE WHOLE WORLD SINGS

STEPHEN FOSTER was born on the Fourth of July in the year 1826. It was the 50th birthday of the United States. Bands were playing and firecrackers popping. Little Stevie was the ninth child of a big family. No one knew that he would be famous.

The Foster family lived in a little town that is now part of Pittsburgh. Tom and Lieve, a black boy and girl, lived with the Fosters. They helped with the work of taking care of a household of children.

Stephen liked music even when he was small. Two-year-old Stephen used to pick at his sister's guitar. He called it his "ittly pizani." Stephen also liked the family's little black and white dog Tray. He did not like to leave Tray at home when he started to school.

In those days schools were very different from schools today. Stephen, only five years old, tried to study the alphabet. Each letter had to be said in a verse. Stephen did not know the meaning of the verse. When the teacher called on him, he started to recite. Then he became scared. He yelled like a little Indian, ran out of the door, and all the way home!

# STEPHEN FOSTER

One day when Stephen and his mother were in a store, the little boy saw a flute. He had never seen a flute before. But Stephen picked it up and played a merry tune! Later Stephen had a flute of his own. He would walk in the woods or along the river, listening to the birds and the many other sounds. Then he would make up his own songs on his flute.

The Fosters moved several times, but always they lived near Pittsburgh. For a while they lived in Allegheny City. They lived near "the Point"—where the Allegheny River and the Monongahela River meet to form the great Ohio River.

Stephen liked to walk along the Ohio River. The steamboats with big paddle wheels brought many things from far-off places down South. Stephen watched the black men as they unloaded the boats. The men sang songs about the cotton and sugar fields. They sang songs of fun and work. Stephen never forgot these songs.

Often, too, Lieve, the black girl who lived with the Fosters, took Stephen to her church. Stephen liked to hear the blacks sing. He remembered those songs, too.

"Stephen Foster, I believe you go to church just to hear the singing!" Lieve teased on Sunday.

"Oh, I like the preaching, too," Stephen said. "But, Lieve, where do your people get their songs? They aren't in the hymn books."

"Some we remember, some we make up as we go along. The songs are in our hearts," Lieve told him.

"Some day I am going to make up songs," Stephen told her. "There are songs in my heart too."

When Stephen was thirteen years old, his mother and father began to worry about him.

"He spends too much time with his music!" said Mr. Foster. "No good will come of it. It is not the way to make a living."

"Let me take Stephen with me," brother William suggested. "While I am working in Towanda, he can go to the Athens Academy."

"It might be a good thing for Stephen." Mrs. Foster agreed.

Stephen did not want to leave his home. But he wanted to please his family. So one snowy morning in January, William and the boy started on the trip.

They went in a sleigh drawn by two horses. Mrs. Foster tucked Stephen in with blankets and warm bricks for his feet. It was a wonderful trip. William had many friends. All along the way he and Stephen were warmly welcomed into homes and inns for good meals and to spend the night. At Harrisburg, they called on the

Governor of Pennsylvania, then they went to a concert.

Stephen wasn't happy at school. He was lonely, and he had promised to study and not pay attention to his music.

Before he left school, however, he wrote a piece for four flutes, *The Tioga Waltz*. He and three classmates played the piece at graduation.

When Stephen came home, he and some friends had a secret club. Stephen spent much time at his piano writing songs for the club. The other boys were proud of him.

Stephen was sixteen years old when his first song was published. When he was twenty, he went to work for a brother. During these three years, he wrote *Old Uncle Ned* and *Oh! Susanna* besides other songs. People liked the words and tunes. Before long, Stephen Foster and his songs were famous.

Although he wrote many songs, Stephen was often poor. He wrote a song about the dog he had when he was a little boy—*Old Dog Tray*. He wrote songs about the black people whom he liked to hear sing. You have probably heard *Old Black Joe* and *My Old Kentucky Home*. He wrote *Jeannie with the Light Brown Hair* to his pretty wife.

Stephen Foster lived a long time ago, but his songs will live always. They are songs from his heart—songs of home, love, and friendship—sung by people all over the world.

## WORDS TO KNOW

| | | |
|---|---|---|
| famous | graduation | published |
| firecrackers | guitar | sleigh |
| flute | Harrisburg | Stephen C. Foster |
| friendship | black | United States |

## WORD MEANINGS

| | |
|---|---|
| famous | Very well-known. |
| guitar | A musical instrument with six strings, played with the fingers. |
| published | Printed and offered for sale. |
| sleigh | A sort of carriage on runners for use on snow or ice. |

## THINGS TO DO

1. The best way to remember Stephen Foster is to learn some of his songs. Have a class discussion and decide which ones to learn. Then plan a Stephen Foster program to give in your room or in the auditorium. Have some children tell about Foster's life. Use all the musical talent in your class.

2. Films have been made about the life of Stephen C. Foster which schools may get to show. Perhaps your teacher will arrange this.
3. Can you find a picture of Stephen Foster to show the class?
4. Several children may have Foster records at home that they would like to bring to play in class.
5. You could make up a musical skit from this chapter. Perhaps the scene could be along the Ohio River.

## 18. JAMES BUCHANAN, A BOY WHO BECAME PRESIDENT

STONY BATTER was the strange name of a narrow gap at the foot of North Mountain in southern Pennsylvania. In early days there were no roads through the dense forest to the west. Indian foot trails, leading over the mountains, passed by this place.

It was here that James Buchanan, a young Scotch-Irishman, built two log cabins. One cabin was his home, the other cabin was a trading post or store. The Indians and white traders brought horses loaded with wild animal furs to trade for guns and other things.

The storekeeper married the daughter of a neighboring farmer. Their first child born in the little log cabin was named after his father, James Buchanan. He became the only President of the United States from Pennsylvania. Little Jamie was a chubby, happy little boy. So that Jamie would not get lost in the forest, his mother tied a bell around his neck. Neighbors later told about seeing little Jamie Buchanan wearing a sheep bell!

The Buchanans moved to Mercersburg, about four miles away, when Jamie was seven years old. There Jamie's father had a large store. In the next years, the

Rebuilt birthplace of President James Buchanan, Franklin County

Buchanans became well-to-do. Now there were eleven children in the family and they lived in a large house.

When Jamie started to school, his schoolmates made fun of his pet name. But Jamie Buchanan had strong fists. The children soon stopped teasing him and, with respect, called him "Jim."

When James became a young man, he went to Dickinson College in Carlisle. At first James tried to please the other boys by not behaving well in school. After his first year, he felt ashamed of his bad record. From then on, he was a very good pupil.

After college, James studied to be a lawyer in Lancaster. He became a fine speaker. Taking long walks through the woods, he would say his speeches aloud.

James became engaged to a very rich Lancaster girl named Anne Coleman. For some reason, the engagement was broken. Very soon after this, Anne Coleman died. James was heart-broken. He never married.

James Buchanan served his country in many ways. First, the people of Pennsylvania elected him to be a Congressman who helps to make the laws of the United States. Later, he was sent to England and to Russia as United States Ambassador. Next, he was elected a Senator, and, after this, he became Secretary of State. These were very important jobs for the government.

In 1849 Buchanan bought a country home in Lancaster. He called his home Wheatland. Two children, a niece and a nephew, played about the house. They were orphans from two different families. Although their uncle was strict, they loved him, and he was their hero.

When Buchanan was elected President of the United States, he left his home in Lancaster and went to live in

Wheatland, home of President James Buchanan at Lancaster. Photo by Pennsylvania State Department of Commerce, Harrisburg, Pennsylvania

Washington. Harriet Lane, the little girl who had made her home with Uncle James, was now a lovely young lady. She became the mistress of the White House. The nephew, James Buchanan Henry, became the private secretary of the President.

These were the days just before the War Between the States. As President, James Buchanan had many problems. After Buchanan's years in office were over, Abraham Lincoln was elected President.

James Buchanan was almost seventy years old when he became President, although he seemed much younger. He spent the rest of his life at his home, Wheatland, in Lancaster. This beautiful house is now open to visitors. Perhaps some day you will visit Wheatland, walk through its handsome rooms, and remember the President from Pennsylvania.

# JAMES BUCHANAN

## WORDS TO KNOW

| | | |
|---|---|---|
| Ambassador | Lancaster | orphan |
| Congressman | lawyer | Secretary of State |
| dense | Mercersburg | Senator |
| elected | neighbor | Stony Batter |
| James Buchanan | | Wheatland |

## WORD MEANINGS

| | |
|---|---|
| dense | Thick. |
| elected | Chosen by a vote of people. |
| orphan | A child who has lost one or two parents by death. |

## THINGS TO DO

1. If you live near Lancaster, plan to visit President Buchanan's home, Wheatland.
2. If you live near Chambersburg, plan to visit James Buchanan State Forest Park to see the little log cabin where the President from Pennsylvania was born.
3. You might like to try to learn the names of the Presidents in the order in which they served the United States.

4. Plan a trip to Washington. You will want to visit the White House, the home of United States Presidents.
5. Don't forget to paint or crayon a little log cabin on your map of Pennsylvania to show where Buchanan was born.
6. From what country did the Scotch-Irish come? Why did they come to Pennsylvania?
7. There were several governors of Pennsylvania who had Scotch-Irish ancestors. Can you find out their names?
8. Who were the first people to build log cabins in this country?
9. Make cardboard models of the different kinds of houses built in Pennsylvania during the early days.

## 19.  GEORGE WESTINGHOUSE, A GREAT INVENTOR

"WHAT HAS stopped the train?" George Westinghouse asked the railroad conductor. "We have been standing here for some time."

"We have some trouble, young man," replied the conductor. "The track must be cleared before we can go ahead. Two freight trains have bumped into each other."

George left the car of the train and walked farther along the tracks. Soon he saw the wrecked freight trains.

"I saw the train coming toward me," said one of the engineers, "I set the hand brakes, but there wasn't time to stop the cars."

"If only the cars could be stopped by the engineer from his engine cab!" said another trainman. "If that could be done, the trains would not have been wrecked."

"What do you mean?" George asked.

"When I want to stop the train," the engineer told him, "I blow the whistle as a signal. There is a brakeman riding on top of each car. When the brakeman hears the whistle, he works the brake. Every car must be braked.

A train cannot be stopped in a moment. If the brakes could be worked by the engineer from his cab, it would save time and lives."

Ever since he was a little boy, George had liked machines. When he had not been in school, he had been busy in his father's machine shop.

George worked on the idea for a brake in his free time. He worked all day in his father's factory in New York State. George liked to read, too. In a magazine he found an idea to make his brake work by air.

George was sure that his air brake would work. His father, who made many machines, did not think so. George took his idea to one railroad office after another. No railroad man would listen to him.

"You think that you can stop a speeding train by air, do you?" they laughed.

George did not give up. He went to see Andrew Carnegie in Pittsburgh. Mr. Carnegie decided to try George's brake.

In September 1868, the air brake was tested on an engine of a train with four cars. This train ran between Pittsburgh and Steubenville, Ohio. Near Union Station at Pittsburgh, the train came out of a tunnel. There was a farmer with his horse and wagon on the tracks! The engineer put on the air brake. The train stopped! It stopped so suddenly that it threw the people in the cars from their seats!

The air brake was tried many times. Each time the air brake worked. In a few weeks George Westinghouse was called one of the great inventors in the world. He was only twenty-two years old. Because of the air brake, trains now could run faster than before. The air brake made traveling on a railroad much safer. It saved many lives.

The success of his air brake made George Westinghouse a very rich young man. But he did not stop working. One of the things he made was a railroad "frog." This "frog" is used to guide the wheels of a railroad car where two tracks meet or cross.

After Westinghouse married, he moved to Pittsburgh. In 1884 he drilled a well for natural gas. The gas was piped to the city for use in homes, mills, and factories. Westinghouse was also the man who learned how to use the water power of Niagara Falls to make electricity. He invented many electrical things for use in the home. When he was an old man, he was still busy with plans.

George Westinghouse had lots of ideas. He worked and studied to learn how to use these ideas. Perhaps there are many boys like him in Pennsylvania today.

## WORDS TO KNOW

| | | |
|---|---|---|
| brake | George Westinghouse | Niagara Falls |
| conductor | inventor | signal |
| engineer | machines | success |
| factory | magazine | whistle |
| | natural gas | |

## WORD MEANINGS

brake     Anything used to slow or stop a machine by pressing or rubbing.

engineer     A man who makes, takes care of, or runs engines.

inventor     A person who makes or thinks out something new.

signal     A sign.

## THINGS TO DO

1. Form a committee interested in science and make a report on air brakes—where they are used and how they work.
2. Use your library to find a list of Westinghouse's inventions and ideas.
3. What things are made today by the company that has his name?

# PART III

# THE STRUGGLE OF THE BLACK MAN

## 20. BEGINNINGS OF SLAVERY AND THE SLAVE TRADE

IN THE early days of Pennsylvania, very few blacks lived here. The first blacks to see America were brought on ships from the countries of Europe. It is believed that there was a black sailor with Christopher Columbus. He was Pedro Alonso Nina. There were other blacks with other explorers.

The first blacks to settle in America were brought from Holland to Jamestown, Virginia. The captain of the ship offered to trade twenty black servants to the settlers in return for food. These blacks worked for a number of years, then became free men.

Today many blacks live in Pennsylvania. They are descendants of people who once lived in Africa. Most of the blacks were brought to America against their will. They came here as slaves.

Hundreds of years ago, Africa was made up of kingdoms. Some of the African kings and their nobles were rich and civilized. Most of the Africans, however, lived very simply. They ate wild animals and raised crops for food. Some of the Africans were skilled in arts, such as wood carvings and working with gold.

# BEGINNINGS OF SLAVERY

The people of some tribes were tall, others were short. Some were light-skinned, others were dark. Each tribe had its own language, manners, and customs.

There was slavery in Africa from earliest times. The black kings had black slaves. A slave may have been captured from another tribe, or a person may have been made a slave because he did something wrong. A king had only a few slaves, and they were treated as members of the family.

Later, men from the countries of Europe bought some slaves from the African kings. Sometimes the African kings made war on villages and captured men and women. Then they sold them to the white slave traders. In return, the African kings were paid such things as tobacco, guns, cloth, and rum.

Slavery was not a new idea. Thousands of years before, the Egyptians had made slaves of the Jewish people. The Jews had slaves too, often other Jews. The Greeks and Romans had slaves, often of their own kind. White people as well as black have been sold into slavery.

In 1637, the first American-built slave ship sailed from New England. After that first time, many slave ships sailed from the American colonies to Africa and back. With a cargo of slaves, a trader sailed from Africa to the West Indies. There he may have sold some slaves.

He took on a load of molasses. Next, the ship stopped at a port in a southern American colony. At this place, the rest of the slaves were sold. Then the ship sailed for the home port of New England. There the molasses was made into rum. With a load of rum, the ship sailed back to Africa to get more slaves.

The trip from Africa was a terrible time of pain and sorrow for the captured blacks. Chained together, they would be forced to walk perhaps for days, to the place where the ship waited. They were given little food or water. They were packed into the hold of the ship, below the deck. Families were separated. Sometimes, babies were taken from their mothers and thrown overboard. The slave traders thought the babies would probably die on the trip, anyhow. Still chained, the blacks had to sit close together; they could hardly move. There was not room to stand. There was little fresh air, and little food or water. Because of this, many blacks died. Some took their own lives rather than become slaves.

When a slave ship arrived at a port of a southern American colony, an auction was held. Each black was sold to the man who bid the most money. Most of the slaves were bought to work on the plantations of the South. The landholders thought they had to have slaves to work in the cotton, sugar, rice, and tobacco fields. Other slaves worked as house servants. Thousands of

# BEGINNINGS OF SLAVERY

black slaves were sold in the colonies every year.

The blacks of a southern plantation lived in little cabins near the big house of the master. Most plantations had no more than twenty slaves but some had hundreds. Some masters were cruel, others were kind. The whip was used often to get the most work out of the slaves. Some blacks learned a trade, but very few were given a chance to learn to read and write. By the late 1600s and early 1700s, some slaves had revolted against their masters. Then the colonists made harsh laws against all blacks. Some people were afraid that the free blacks would lead the slaves to revolt.

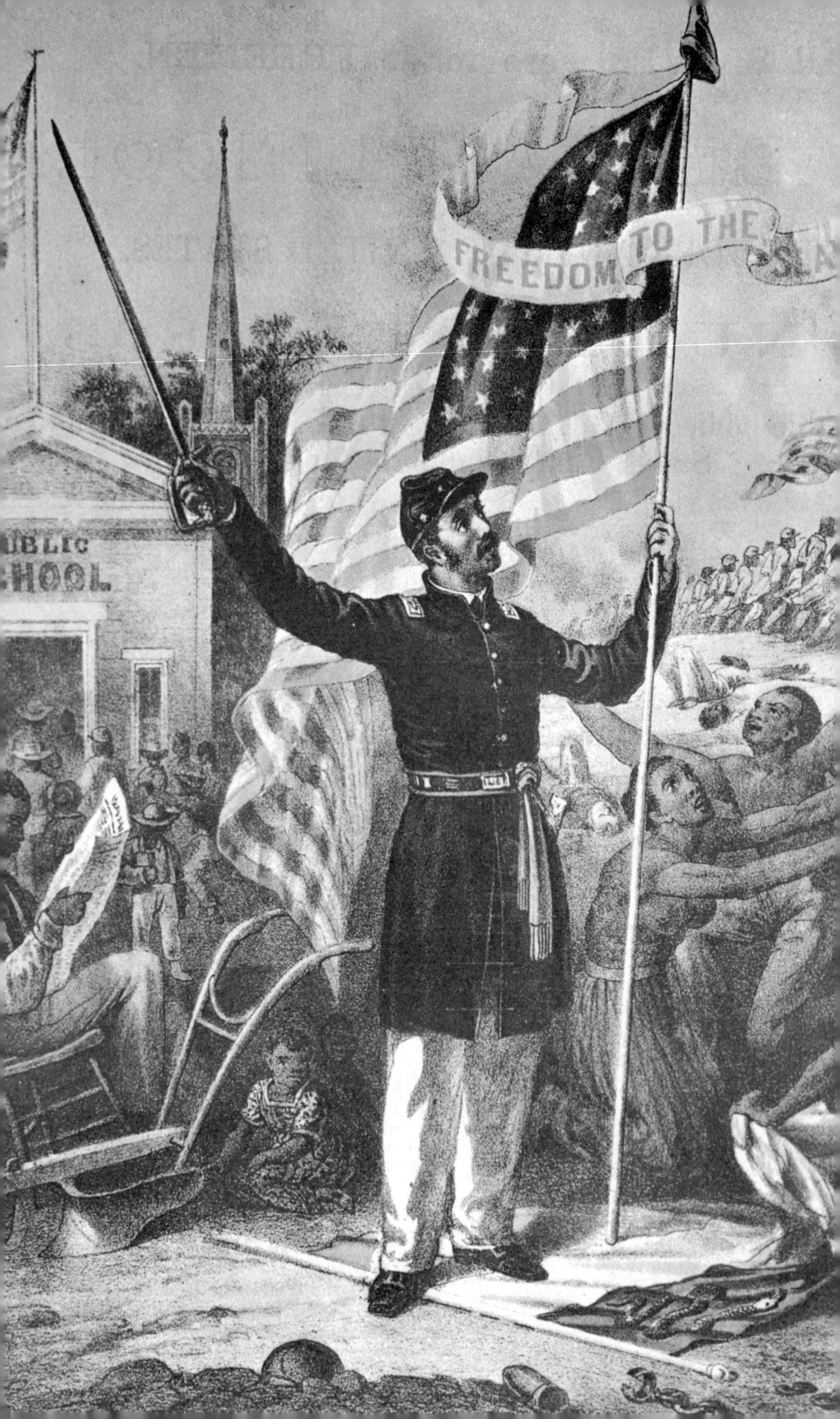
FREEDOM TO THE SLA
UBLIC
HOOL

## 21. SLAVERY IN PENNSYLVANIA AND THE NEW NATION

IN EARLY America few white people thought it was wrong to have slaves. In 1688, a group of men in Germantown made the first public protest against slavery. Their reasons against slavery were read aloud at a Friends meeting.

William Penn, founder of Pennsylvania, knew that slavery was wrong. He asked that his few slaves be set free after he died. This was not done, however.

In 1733, Benjamin Rush, a doctor who lived in Germantown, said that no more slaves should be brought into this country. But thousands of black slaves continued to be sold to the American colonies each year.

Pennsylvania did set a tax on slave owners for each black slave, however. But the reason for this was that owners hired out the slaves for wages that were much less than wages paid to free men. A black brick layer, for example, was paid less than a free white brick layer. And of course the owners usually pocketed the wages that the slave earned. It was to stop this that the tax was made.

An old drawing showing the hopes of black slaves.

Then, in 1780, the government of Pennsylvania passed a new law. It said that no child born in Pennsylvania, of slave parents, should be a slave. The child would be a servant until he was twenty-eight years old, then he or she would be a free man or woman. This was the first step toward ending slavery in the United States.

During the Revolutionary War, about 5,000 blacks were in the army. Some were free men, others were slaves. Crispus Attucks, a black runaway slave, was the first black killed while fighting for this country. The British promised freedom to those who joined the British Army. With this hope, thousands of slaves ran away. No one knows how many joined the British, or how many were caught.

After the Revolutionary War, many great fortunes were made by the American slave traders. But most of the leaders of the new nation were against slavery. Several states, however, would not join the Union unless slavery was allowed.

In 1793, Eli Whitney invented the cotton gin. It was a machine that separated the seeds from the cotton plant. Before, this was done by hand. The southern plantations wanted to grow more cotton. Now they needed even more slaves.

At last a law was passed to stop the bringing of slaves into this country. It became a law on January 1, 1808.

By this time, there were about one million black slaves in the United States.

By then, however, the selling of slaves had become big business. Auction blocks and slave "pens" were common sights on city streets. Black slave families had become larger. It was "good business" to sell children. The price of a slave also became higher. By 1860, a field worker sold for $1,000 in Virginia, or $15,000 in New Orleans, Louisiana. By 1861, about 400,000 slaves lived in cities and towns. They were hired out as tailors, shoemakers, painters, factory workers, carpenters, or house servants. The money they earned was taken by their masters.

But more and more people began to think that slavery was wrong. Many people in the North were against slavery. But if the slaves were freed, where would they go? What would they do?

Some people thought that the blacks should go back to Africa. A society was formed to help blacks return to Africa. During the years of the 1820s and early 1830s about 12,000 blacks did go to Africa. They started the colony of Liberia which became a separate nation. Many more blacks wanted to stay in this country. At times, the slaves revolted, but they could not do much to help themselves. Blacks who became free tried to help others.

Now and then slaves ran away. Sometimes they made their way to the safety of the northern states. Then a law was passed that a runaway slave must be sent back to his master. Some people in the North, especially Quakers and others who thought like them, planned a way to help the slaves to escape. They planned that at certain places a runaway slave could stop for food and lodging. Those places were called stations. Usually, a slave stopped at a station at daylight. At night, he went on until he reached another safe hiding place. This secret way of helping the slaves to escape was called the Underground Railroad. Many people in Pennsylvania helped the slaves to freedom.

An old drawing showing President Lincoln proclaiming the freeing of the slaves

FREEDOM FOR ALL, BOTH BLACK AND WHITE!

## 22. THE BATTLE FOR FREEDOM

THE NORTH and South could not agree about slavery. The South wanted slavery in any part of the United States. The North thought that slavery should be only in those states that already had it.

In 1854 a new law was passed. This law gave any territory the right to vote for or against slavery before joining the Union as a state. There were people who had settled on land called territories. These territories were lands which were not yet settled by enough people to become states. When a territory wanted to join the Union, the people of the territory asked to be admitted as a state. The country was just growing into the United States as we know it today.

This new law brought about the beginning of a new political party—the Republican Party. The Southerners, who were Democrats, feared a new party. They said that if a Republican President was ever elected, the South would leave the Union.

In March, 1861, Abraham Lincoln, a Republican, was elected President; seven southern states left the Union. They formed the Confederate States of America. They elected Jefferson Davis as their President.

# THE BATTLE FOR FREEDOM

Lincoln believed that no state could leave the Union. He sent men and war supplies to Fort Sumter, South Carolina. The Confederates fired on the fort. In this way, the War Between the States began. It is usually called the Civil War because it was between people who belonged to the same nation. There were almost four million black slaves in the United States at this time. Many blacks left the plantations to join the Union Army. At first, these slaves were used as workers, not as soldiers. Later, Lincoln let the blacks join the army. About 185,000 blacks fought for the Union.

In September 1862, Lincoln announced the Emancipation Proclamation. It said that on January 1, 1863, those persons held as slaves in states in rebellion against the United States would be free. The Emancipation Proclamation was not a law, but merely a policy of the Union government. It was not until December 1865, however, that slavery in the United States was really ended by the Thirteenth Amendment to the U.S. Constitution.

No payment was made to the owners of slaves when the blacks were freed. No plans were made as to what would be done with the freed slaves. Lincoln had talked with free black leaders, but nothing had been planned. Some black leaders thought the freed slaves should go to Africa. Others thought the blacks should have a state of their own. No one knew how the freed slaves would make a living.

The War Between the States came to an end in April 1865. The Union had won. When the slaves were freed in December, many stayed on the plantations where they lived. Those with some skills went to towns and cities. Others, with the help of the government, bought farms of their own. One out of every nine Americans was a freed slave. But none were yet citizens. They could not vote, sit on a jury in a court, or hold public office.

Before anything could be decided about what was to be done with the freed slaves, Lincoln was shot by John Wilkes Booth, an actor who had sided with the South. Lincoln was shot in the back of the head as he sat beside his wife watching a play in the Ford Theatre in Washington. He died the next day. Booth was hunted down and shot to death. It was thought that Booth was not really well.

In the South, farmland had been ruined by the war. Homes, plantations, and cities had been burned. The old way of life in the South was gone. Bad times followed. Crops failed, pests destroyed the cotton, and there were floods that ruined the land. The plantation owners became poor. The blacks had even less.

Many groups tried to help the blacks. Some Northerners went to the South to help the blacks learn

# THE BATTLE FOR FREEDOM

skills and to help them get land. The government started schools for the former slaves. The government gave medicine and other things that were needed; it helped start hospitals. During this time, too, many churches were started.

After the war, some blacks were given jobs in offices of the counties, states, and the government in Washington. Some of the blacks were good leaders; others did not have enough education to hold such jobs. The Southerners did not like it that former slaves held these jobs.

Little by little, white Southerners were able to get the blacks out of public offices. Many groups were formed to do just that. One of these groups was the Ku Klux Klan. Members of the Ku Klux Klan wore white sheets and hoods so that no one would know who they were. They burned crosses at night meetings to give warnings to blacks and to frighten them.

When white people of the South came into power again, they made laws against the blacks. Also, the blacks had to stay separate from white people in public places such as schools, dining halls, theatres, buses, and trains.

## 23. THE STRUGGLE FOR DIGNITY

MOST BLACKS stayed in the South even until 1910, fifty years after the War Between the States. Most of these blacks lived on farms. Only a few of these blacks owned land.

In the North, factories began to make many more products. Blacks began to go to the North to get jobs in the factories. Black groups helped.

At the time of World War I (1914-1918), blacks began to move into the cities. As the United States began to make products for the war, there were many more jobs for blacks. It was hard for blacks to find nice homes to live in, however. Often they didn't have enough money to get good houses. Also, many white people did not want blacks to live on the same streets as they did. Because of this, many blacks lived in slums or ghettos.

Thousands of blacks joined the army and navy. Hundreds of these men became officers. Black and white men were still kept separate, however.

After the war, the Ku Klux Klan became stronger. There were members in at least thirty states. They worked against not only blacks, but Catholics, and Jews

# THE STRUGGLE FOR DIGNITY

also. Sometimes the Ku Klux Klan hanged blacks. Fear and hate grew. The black slums became worse. The blacks who lived on farms in the South were very poor.

The Great Depression began in 1929. Businesses failed and millions of people were out of work. In cities and towns, people stood in line to get food to eat. Then Franklin D. Roosevelt became President. The government began to help people who didn't have work. Then more blacks were able to get work as clerks, typists, and in government programs. Mrs. Eleanor Roosevelt, the President's wife, did much to help the blacks.

In December 1941, the Japanese attacked Pearl Harbor. The United States declared war on Japan and entered World War II. Again blacks fought for their country. White and black troops still were kept separate, however. Many blacks became officers in the army and navy. Black women also joined the services.

As more men went into the services, there were more jobs for blacks. Many blacks worked in defense plants that made products for war. Now blacks were paid more nearly the same as white people doing the same kind of work.

After World War II and during the 1940s, blacks began to have more rights as citizens. Every President helped to get these rights. Some new rights came about by law, by "sit-ins," prayings, freedom marches, and other ways. White men and blacks were kept separate no longer in the armed services. Black children started to go to white schools.

Today most blacks live in cities. In some cities, poor housing has been torn down; new homes have been built. More plans are being made for better housing.

It is important that blacks go to good schools and learn new skills so that they can get better jobs and thus improve their way of life. A great effort is being made to see that pre-school children get an early start in learning. More young blacks are in school today than ever before. Thousands go on to college. Many go on to more schooling. Black leaders also are teaching people of their race how to own and run businesses. All this means a better future for everyone, white and black. But we all have still a lot to learn about how to live together.

## Chapters 20-23

### WORDS TO KNOW

| | | |
|---|---|---|
| Abraham Lincoln | Eli Whitney | Greeks |
| Africa | Emancipation | Ku Klux Klan |
| Crispus Attucks | Proclamation | plantation |
| customs | Europe | Romans |
| dignity | Franklin D. | Underground |
| Egyptian | Roosevelt | Railroad |

### WORD MEANINGS

| | |
|---|---|
| auction | A sale in which goods or property are sold to the person who offers the most money for them. |
| molasses | A thick brown syrup that drains from sugar as it is being made. |
| servant | A person hired by another person to serve his personal or family needs. |
| prejudice | A dislike of others for unfair reasons. |
| rights | Conditions that a person feels are due to him and others so that he can live decently and in freedom. |

## THINGS TO DO

1. Listen to records of negro spirituals. Ask your music teacher to help you learn an old slave song. Are these songs like the "soul music" of today?
2. Read about the life of Abraham Lincoln. Some children may tell about his boyhood, others about his life as a young man, and still others about his years as President.
3. Draw and color the United States flag as it was during the Civil War.
4. Plan a bulletin board. Use pictures and clippings of blacks in the news today. Use pictures of blacks in the government, the civil rights movement, athletes, entertainers, teachers, etc. Discuss what they have done.
5. Invite a black leader from your community to give a talk to your class.
6. Make a report on Eli Whitney.
7. Show the route of a slave ship on a map.
8. Make up a play about the Underground Railroad. Some of the people in the play might be Harriet Tubman, slaves, and Quakers.
9. Here is a list of famous blacks who were born in Pennsylvania. How many do you know?
    Harry T. Burleigh — singer
    Marian Anderson — singer

# THE STRUGGLE FOR DIGNITY 177

Raymond Pace Alexander — judge
Jessie Fauset — writer
Meta Warrick Fuller — sculptor
Alaine Leroy Locke — writer
Horace Pippin — painter
Henry O. Tanner — painter
Dr. Daniel H. Williams — surgeon
Matthew Anderson — minister
Bill Cosby — comedian, actor, and leader

## FOR THE TEACHERS

## FILMS:

**African Craftsmen: The Ashanti**
  11 min. color Produced by Frank Gardonyi and Clifford Janoff 1970
**African Heritage**
  29 min. color University of Pennsylvania Museum
**Booker T. Washington**
  18 min. EBF 1951
**George Washington Carver**
  12 min. color Artisan 1959
**The Lady From Philadelphia**
  60 min. Produced for the Edward R. Murrow television program "See It Now", December, 1957
**Marian Anderson**
  27 min. Mills Picture Corp. 1953
**The Negro In Pennsylvania History**
  25 min. Pa. Dept. of Public Instruction, 1966

**The Legend of John Henry**
11 min. color Stephen Bosustow Productions, Santa Monica, California
**The Magic Tree**
10 min. color Produced and Directed by Gerald McDermott 1970 Texture Films
**A Story, A Story**
10 min. color Weston Woods 1973
**Anansi The Spider: A Tale From The Ashanti**
10 min. color African Folklore Series, no. 1 1969 Weston Woods

## RECORDS

**Black Man In America** Credo 1
**To Be A Slave** Caedmon TC 2066
**Black Pioneers In American History; v. 1 & 2** Caedmon TC 1252 TC1299
**Up From Slavery: Booker T. Washington** CMS-540
**Life And Times of Frederick Douglas** CMS-570
**Autobiography of Frederick Douglas** Folkways FH 5522
**Walk Together Children** (read and sung by Vinnie Burrows) Spoken Arts SA-1030-v. 1
**Negro Folk Music of Africa and America** Folkways FE 4500
**Negro Woman** FH 5523
**African Folk Tales v. I & II** (told by Bertha Parker) CMS Records CMS-547 CMS-550
**African Village Folktales v. I & II** Caedmon TC-1309 TC-1310

## FILMSTRIPS

**Black Leaders of The 20th Century America** International Book Corporation 1970 Distributed by Holt, Rinehart & Winston, Inc. (10 filmstrips and 5 records)
**Social History of Black Americans** Holt, Rinehart & Winston, Inc. (6 filmstrips)
**John Henry: An American Legend** Guidance Associates 14 min. These teaching materials are recommended by The Free Library of Philadelphia, Office of Work with Children.

Organizations to write to for more material:
Association for the Study of Negro Life and History,
1407 14th Street, N. W., Washington, DC 20005
  A. Speakers
  B. Materials for curriculum development.
The Harmon Foundation,
598 Madison Avenue, New York, NY 10022
  A. Information on Negro Art
  B. Filmstrips
  C. Pictures of outstanding Negroes

Bill Cosby, comedian, actor, and leader from Philadelphia

# PART IV

# THE LAND AND THE PEOPLE

# 24. OLD AND NEW WAYS OF TRAVEL IN PENNSYLVANIA

THE INDIANS had many footpaths through the forests of Pennsylvania. They walked or rode horseback over the trails. They traveled the creeks and rivers in canoes.

At first the settlers who had come across the seas in big sailing ships, used the Indian trails or went by boat. But the settlers wanted a better way to travel. They cut down trees and cleared a way for roads. The first roads were dirt roads. They were dusty in summer and muddy when it rained. Horses splashed right through creeks. There were no bridges!

After the War of Independence, "corduroy" roads were built. If the dirt road went through swampy, wet places, narrow tree trunks were laid cross-wise on the road. This made a rough road because the tree trunks were round and not flat. This kind of a road looked like the ridges in corduroy cloth; that's why it was called a corduroy road. But it was very uncomfortable to travel on.

The first good road in America was the Lancaster Turnpike. It cost a lot of money to build this road. So the company that built the road decided to collect money, or tolls, from the travelers.

At a certain place, a long wooden pole was put across the road to stop the traveler. This pole was called a "pike." At the pole, the traveler had to pay a toll. Then the pole was turned out of the way, and the traveler went on his journey. Because of the pole or pike, this road was called a *turnpike*. Today, any highway on which the traveler has to pay a toll is still called a turnpike.

In early days people traveled in wagons, carriages, or stagecoaches drawn by horses. To ride in a stagecoach, you paid a fare. Conestoga wagons also used the roads. A Conestoga wagon was very large, and almost boat-shaped, high at front and back and low in the center. It was built like this so that a load of goods would not shift to front or back while going over the hills. Hoops were fastened to the body of the wagon and covered with white canvas. The wagon was drawn by six or eight horses. The first covered wagon was built in the Conestoga Valley of Pennsylvania. Many people traveled to the west in Conestoga wagons.

Soon more turnpikes were built. But people didn't like to pay so much money to travel on the turnpikes. They wanted a cheaper way to travel. Men remembered that in countries across the ocean, there were canals for travel.

# OLD AND NEW WAYS OF TRAVEL

A canal is a waterway through land. It is built by men. A canal boat had no engine. Horses or mules pulled or towed a canal boat by a long rope. They walked on a path called the towpath beside the canal. A man at the back or stern guided the boat with a rudder. A boy drove the horses. A canal boat went three or four miles an hour.

Many canals were built in Pennsylvania. The Pennsylvania Canal went from Columbia to Pittsburgh. Then people could travel by water to the new land in the west.

Canal boats carrying passengers were called packet boats. Coal, lumber, food, and other things could be sent by freight boats to towns along the canal.

At this time, a canal boat was not the only way to travel. There were a few railroads in Pennsylvania. The cars were pulled on wooden tracks by horses.

On rivers, boats were used. The flat boats were large rafts made of logs. Men with long poles and a man at the big rudder guided a flat boat. Often a small cabin was built on the boat.

John Fitch, a Pennsylvanian, invented the steamboat. His steamboat made a trip down the Delaware River. But no one thought that a steamboat really could be used.

Robert Fulton, who was born in Little Britain, Pennsylvania, believed that a steamboat was a wonderful idea. He built a steamboat he called *The Clermont*. It had a steam engine, paddle wheels at both sides, and a place for sails, too! People made fun of Robert Fulton. They called his steamboat "Fulton's Folly."

One day in 1807, however, the *Clermont* went up the Hudson River from New York City all the way to Albany at a speed of about five miles an hour! People all along the way stared in wonder. They had never seen a boat go

A canal boat yard of olden times

without sails! Robert Fulton proved that a steamboat could be a success.

Then people in America began to think about using steam to run trains. Over in England, steam locomotives were being made. An English-made locomotive was sent to Pennsylvania. It had a lion's head painted on the front of the engine. The locomotive was at Honesdale. People came from miles around to see the engine go.

"It won't start!" a man shouted.

"Watch out! It will blow up!" cried another.

But the Lion did go. It rattled over the tracks at ten miles an hour! In those days, that was a great speed! This was the first time a locomotive was run in the New World.

Mathias W. Baldwin, a Philadelphia watchmaker, built the first train to run in Pennsylvania. He built the locomotive and the cars. The locomotive was called "Old Ironsides." This train ran between Philadelphia and Norristown for twenty years. Baldwin built a factory where thousands of locomotives have been made.

Passengers were jolted badly on these early trains. Black smoke and hot cinders poured from the engine. Passengers often carried open umbrellas to keep off the smoke and cinders. Sometimes the umbrellas caught fire! But in 1833 it was wonderful to go sixteen miles an hour!

PA State Dept. of Commerce
The Stourbridge Lion, oldest locomotive in Pennsylvania

Before long, however, both trains and tracks were made in a better way. More railroads were built. By 1852 people could go by rail all the way from Harrisburg to Pittsburgh. This way of travel was much faster than by packet boat. It was a much faster way to send coal, lumber, and other things, too. After awhile, canals were no longer used very much.

PA State Dept. of Commerce
A modern complex of highways in Pennsylvania

Today people travel the roads by automobile or bus. They travel by steam and electric railroads, trolley, subway and elevated train; by boat, and by airplane. Travel is much easier and more pleasant than it was years ago.

If you travel through the state by automobile, you may go on the Pennsylvania Turnpike. It is built from Philadelphia to the state of Ohio. This road is sometimes called the Dream Highway because it was built to make driving easy, swift, and safe. There are no steep hills or sharp curves. No roads cross the highway; bridges above the road are built for other travelers. There are many signs to help the driver. Fences on both sides of the road keep farm and wild animals from getting on the turnpike.

Tunnels for the road were made through seven mountains! Each tunnel is about a mile long. Pennsylvania has many fine roads. But the Turnpike was the greatest of all when it was built, and was the first of its kind in America. Today other equally great highways cross our state.

## WORDS TO KNOW

| | | |
|---|---|---|
| canal | Lancaster Turnpike | rudder |
| carriage | locomotive | steam |
| Conestoga wagon | Mathias Baldwin | swampy |
| corduroy | Pennsylvania | *The Clermont* |
| freight | Turnpike | railroads |
| tolls | John Fitch | Robert Fulton |
| | tunnel | |

# OLD AND NEW WAYS OF TRAVEL

## WORD MEANINGS

freight  The goods that are shipped to other places by ships, planes, trains, trucks, etc.

locomotive  Railroad engine.

rudder  A movable piece at the rear of a boat by which it is steered.

swampy  Land that is soft and wet.

tunnel  An underground passage.

## THINGS TO DO

1. After you have studied this chapter, use the information you learned and plan a program for another room, or for the whole school. Assign different children to tell about corduroy roads, the Conestoga wagon, canals, early railroads, river rafts, Fulton's steamboat, etc. You can make drawings and models to use during the program. Read Jane Flory's book "A Tune for a Towpath."
2. You can learn a lot more about early travel from books and pictures in the library.
3. Does anyone in your class collect models of old cars, boats, or locomotives as a hobby? Ask them to bring them to school.

4. The William Penn Memorial Museum at Harrisburg and other museums in Pennsylvania have fine collections of stagecoaches, covered wagons, and carriages. Plan to go to see them.
5. On the class map of Pennsylvania mark the route of the Pennsylvania Canal.
6. Perhaps someone in the class would like to tell about Indian trails and the famous Appalachian Trail.
7. Mark the route of the Delaware Canal on the map of Pennsylvania. Part of this canal is in Roosevelt State Park. During the summer you can take a ride on a barge drawn by mules along this canal. Has anyone in the class taken this ride?

## 25.  HOW PEOPLE LIVE AND WORK IN PENNSYLVANIA

LET'S LOOK at a map of Pennsylvania. See how we can divide our state into three parts: the east, the central, and the west. See the extra piece of land up at the left hand corner. Do you think it looks something like a chimney? It is sometimes called the "chimney corner" of Pennsylvania. On the right is the Delaware River. It makes a wavy line which is the eastern boundary line of Pennsylvania.

### EASTERN PENNSYLVANIA

Philadelphia is on the Delaware River. This is the city that William Penn, the founder of Pennsylvania, planned. Penn's "green country town" is now the largest city in the state. It is one of the largest cities in the United States. There are still small parks in the city as Penn planned. There is also Fairmount Park, which is the largest city park in the United States.

In the center of downtown Philadelphia is City Hall. It looks like a palace. On top of the tower stands a giant statue of William Penn. Sometimes Philadelphia is called "The Quaker City." Near City Hall is a new shopping center, new office buildings, and apartment houses.

In other parts of the city, houses unfit for homes have been torn down. New houses have been built in their place. Philadelphia is sometimes called "the city of homes." Many people live in long rows of houses; others live in big or little houses in small towns near the city.

Some people work in offices or stores. Others work in factories. Hundreds of differnt products are made in Philadelphia. Some of these things are textiles, such as stockings, carpet, silk and rayon yarns, dresses, coats, and shirts. Philadelphia is also famous for the making of ice cream. There are large petroleum and sugar refineries, too.

Because the city is on the Delaware River, goods can be sent by ship down the river to the ocean and to all parts of the world. Thousands of ships from many countries load and unload at the docks. Railroads take goods from other towns and cities to and from the port.

A little to the north of Philadelphia is Levittown, where thousands of small homes have been built. Some of the people who live there work at the Fairless Steel plant.

# HOW PEOPLE LIVE AND WORK

Nearby is beautiful farmland, old towns and villages where actors, artists, and writers live. New Hope on the Delaware River is a famous artists' colony.

Look at your map again. Find the city of Bethlehem. Here is one of the largest steel plants in the state. The city of Allentown lies next to Bethlehem. Allentown is a manufacturing city.

Going farther north, see how the Delaware River has cut a gorge through the mountains at Delaware Water Gap. This part of our state, Stroudsburg and all through the Pocono Mountains, is vacation land.

Now find Reading, south of Allentown, on your map. Reading is famous for the making of hosiery, hats, and pretzels. South of Reading is Lancaster. Clothes and linoleum are made in this city. There are wonderful farmers' markets, too.

Now find Harrisburg on your map. Harrisburg is the capital of Pennsylvania. It is on the Susquehanna River. The state capitol buildings are magnificent. Here the laws of the state are made. In Capitol Park is a state library and a beautiful concert hall called the Forum. When you visit Harrisburg, be sure to visit the William Penn Memorial Museum. Nearby is the Archives Building where records about the state are kept.

Close to Harrisburg is Hershey, the famous town where chocolate is made. Hershey is a place to enjoy.

PA State Dept. of Commerce
Part of the State Capitol at Harrisburg

# HOW PEOPLE LIVE AND WORK

There is a sports arena, amusement park, rose gardens, a theatre, a stadium, a fine hotel, a zoo, and an Indian museum.

North of Harrisburg are the coal fields. This is the area around Scranton, Hazelton, and Wilkes-Barre. Coal mining, however, is no longer big business. Other fuels such as oil are used instead of anthracite or hard coal. Some years ago, many coal mines were closed. There were no more jobs. Many people moved away. Other people did not have the money to move. They had a hard time trying to earn a living.

Then, near the end of World War II, a man came into the Scranton area looking for a place to make army tents. This meant jobs. He and another man spent their own money to build a factory; people were hired to make tents. It was the beginning of bringing new kinds of work to people in the coal mining country.

Today Scranton's Keystone Industrial Park is a model for building factories in a park-like place. Many jobs for workers have been made. People in other coal mining areas decided to do the same thing. Pottsville, Wilkes-Barre, and Hazelton all have new industries. New roads led to these cities and to the big cities of New York, Boston, Philadelphia, and others. Northeastern Pennsylvania has a new look.

## SOUTH CENTRAL PENNSYLVANIA

Now find south central Pennsylvania on your map. Find Gettysburg. One of the greatest battles in the War Between the States was fought here. You can visit the battlefield today.

Nearby is Caledonia State Park, one of the many parks cared for by the state. People can picnic, go swimming, fishing, or boating in the state parks. There are cabins to rent and places for tents and trailers.

In the country between York Springs and Chambersburg there are many apple and peach orchards. Apple Blossom Day is celebrated the first Sunday in May.

## CENTRAL PENNSYLVANIA

In the central part of our state, the land looks much like it did when the first settlers came. In the forests of the "Endless Mountains" are many deer, black bears, and wild turkeys. Every year in early August, a Woodsmen's Carnival is held in Cherry Springs State Park near Coudersport.

# HOW PEOPLE LIVE AND WORK

Look at Wellsboro near the top of the map. Here Pine Creek cuts right through the mountains. This beautiful place is called the "Grand Canyon of Pennsylvania." It is in Harrison State Park.

The town of State College is almost in the very center of our state. The Pennsylvania State University is there. Nearby is Philipsburg, sometimes regarded as having the coldest winter weather in the state. The mountains in this part of the state contain the most and largest caves in the state. The city of Altoona was famous once for its great railroad workshops. And the great Horseshoe Curve of the former Penn Central Railroad just west of Altoona is known far and wide.

Near Somerset, maple trees are tapped for sap. Maple syrup and maple candy are made. Every year a Maple Syrup Festival is held.

## WESTERN PENNSYLVANIA

The Allegheny Mountains separate the central part of our state from the western part. In southwestern Pennsylvania are the bituminous, or soft coal, mines. There

"The Golden Triangle" at Pittsburgh

State Dept. of Commerce

are cities where iron and steel are made. Pittsburgh is one of the world's largest steel-making cities. It also leads in the making of aluminum, plate and window glass, air brakes, and other products.

Pittsburgh is the second largest city in Pennsylvania. The city has grown up where the Monongahela and Allegheny Rivers meet to form the Ohio River. Many, many boats carry goods up and down these rivers. There

## HOW PEOPLE LIVE AND WORK

are many factories along the shores. And there are over a hundred bridges in Pittsburgh!

The point of land where the Monogahela and the Allegheny Rivers meet to form the Ohio River is in downtown Pittsburgh. This point of land is called "the Golden Triangle." The city began at this place in 1758 as a fort and a village. Fort Pitt Blockhouse, built by the British, still stands in Point State Park.

At one time, Pittsburgh was a dirty, sooty city. The many factories made the air unfit to breathe. People had to wash the inside walls of their houses several times a year. The word "smog" (smoke and fog) was first used in Pittsburgh, "the Smoky City." Now Pittsburgh is a cleaner city with a smoke control and flood control program. Home-owners must use smokeless fuel. The railroads use Diesel-electric locomotives. Industries use smoke filters.

Pittsburgh is a center of education. There are three universities and other fine schools and important museums.

In the northwestern part of the state is Pymatuning Lake. Here the state has made a safe place for wild water birds to come and stay.

Cook Forest is another wonderful state park to visit. Some of the forest here has never been cut or burned over. There are white pine trees as tall as a 17-story building. There are hemlock trees four or five feet around.

Nearby is Allegheny National Forest. Here, too, many of the trees have never been cut. It is a wonderful place to walk, picnic, and camp.

Now find Warren on the map. Nine miles above Warren is one of the largest man-made bodies of water in the eastern part of our country. It is the lake created by the Kinzua Dam.

Look on your map again. Find the "chimney corner" of Pennsylvania. Grapes, apples, and peaches are raised here. Every year there is a Grape Festival in the old town of North East.

This "chimney corner" is the only part of the state that was not given to William Penn by King Charles II. Because Pennsylvania had no port on Lake Erie, state leaders wanted to buy land here so that a Pennsylvania port on the Great Lakes could be created. This "chimney corner" piece of land was claimed by the states of New York, Massachusetts, and Connecticut. In 1792, the United States paid these states for their claims. Then Pennsylvania paid the national government for the money spent. Pennsylvania also paid the Indians for their rights to the land. The name Erie comes from the Erie Indians who once lived here.

The city of Erie is on Lake Erie. It is the third largest city in the state. Erie is an important port. Lake boats bring loads of iron ore and grain to the city. It is not only a lake port. Since the opening of the Seaway which links the Great Lakes with the Atlantic Ocean, it is also a sea port. Large ocean-going ships unload products from foreign lands.

Many different products are made in Erie, mostly metal products such as machinery, furniture, and other things.

Presque Isle State Park is the peninsula that juts out into Lake Erie and forms the Erie Harbor. Much of Lake Erie, however, has been polluted badly by city and industry wastes draining into it. Thus fishing and swimming are no longer as popular along its shores. Many people now are working to correct that.

Pennsylvania has big cities, small towns, and beautiful farmland. There are rivers, lakes, mountains, and forests. There are so many highways in our state that if they were all one road, it would go four times around the world! Everywhere you go, all through the state, there are metal markers along the road to tell you the historical stories of Pennsylvania.

Best of all are the many different kinds of people who have helped to make the story of our state. Today, you too are a part of this story.

## WORDS TO KNOW

| | | |
|---|---|---|
| Allegheny | education | offices |
| anthracite | Erie | pollution |
| bituminous | Fairmount Park | Reading |
| boundary | Gettysburg | Seaway |
| capital | Grand Canyon | Scranton |
| central | Harrisburg | Somerset |
| Chambersburg | hemlock | Susquehanna |
| chimney | Hershey | tobacco |
| chocolate | iron | university |
| eastern | linoleum | Wilkes-Barre |

## WORD MEANINGS

| | |
|---|---|
| anthracite | Hard coal. |
| bitum-inous | Soft coal. |
| capital | City where the government of a country or state is located. |
| iron | The strong metal from which steel is made. |
| pollution | Wastes — smoke, garbage, dumps, certain chemicals, etc. — which make places unhealthy or unfit. |

## THINGS TO DO

1. On the map of Pennsylvania, draw small pictures that will help you remember some of the cities and towns you learned about in this chapter. Example: a chocolate bar for Hershey, or the tall chimneys of the steel mills in Pittsburgh. This will make your map a real picture map.
2. Plan a class trip to the state capitol, a factory, a large store, state park, farm, farmers' market, or a place famous in Pennsylvania history.
3. Do you know a man or woman who works in a place that makes a Pennsylvania product? Ask that person to come and talk to your class.
4. Make a list of Pennsylvania products. Make a list of products made in your town.
5. Do you use anything in your classroom that is made in Pennsylvania? Do you wear any clothes that are made in our state?

## 26. SYMBOLS OF OUR STATE

THERE ARE two flags that fly over the state capitol buildings. One is the flag of the United States. The other is the blue state flag. In the center of the state flag is a picture. The ship in the picture tells that Pennsylvania sends things to all parts of the world. The plow and the corn tell that Pennsylvania is a farming state.

PA State Dept. of Commerce
The Pennsylvania state flag

# SYMBOLS OF OUR STATE

The olive branch shows that the people of Pennsylvania love peace.

Every state in our country has chosen a flower to be the state flower. Pennsylvania has chosen the mountain laurel, a wild flower. The blossoms are white or pinkish. In the spring, you can see the mountain laurel blooming on the hillsides.

The ruffed grouse is the state bird. It is reddish brown with dark markings. This bird makes its nest on the ground. It helps the farmers by eating insects. When the snow is deep, it buries in the snow to keep warm until morning. The ruffed grouse stays in our state all summer and winter.

The hemlock is the state tree of Pennsylvania. It is a tall, beautiful evergreen tree. The mountains of our state are filled with hemlock trees.

The whitetail deer is the state animal. There are many deer in Pennsylvania.

The state dog is the great dane.

The state insect is the firefly.

## WORDS TO KNOW

| capitol | mountain laurel | ruffed grouse |
| hemlock | olive branch | symbol |

## WORD MEANINGS

capital  The city where the government of a state or nation is conducted.

PA Historical and Museum Commission
The William Penn Memorial Museum and State Archives at Harrisburg

# SYMBOLS OF OUR STATE

capitol     Building where the government of a country or state is located.

symbol     Something that suggests or stands for a set of ideas or things.

## THINGS TO DO

1. In the margin of the Pennsylvania map, draw the state symbols—the flag, flower, bird, and tree. Perhaps a committee of the class interested in art would like to do this.
2. Sometimes laurel leaves are used as a symbol, too. For what?
3. Learn to identify the hemlock. Can you name other evergreen trees that grow in Pennsylvania?
4. Look in a book or magazine to find the flag and flower of another state.
5. Find out how the firefly came to be the state insect.
6. Make a chart of all the important dates in the history of Pennsylvania, beginning with 1681 when King Charles II signed the charter granting William Penn the land. Make the chart for room display.

PA State Dept. of Commerce
The ruffed grouse, state bird of Pennsylvania